The Pit of Despair

Praise for *The Pit of Despair*

Life can be hard on any given day, but let's add addiction to the mix and it can become so overwhelming that it's easier to spin out of control. A strong support system is critical, including learning to open the lines of communication to the 'Big Guy' himself. Lisa Jo speaks from the heart, and from experience, while encouraging others to reflect and participate in their own recovery. *The Pit of Despair* is an inspiration and a reminder that not all is lost–even in the darkest of times.

Jeffrey Hayzlett—Primetime TV & Podcast Host,
Speaker, Author and Part-Time Cowboy

Lisa Jo's life story is a beautiful and powerful example of "With man this is impossible, but with God all things are possible." Her book is a bright shining light in a world darkened by addiction and suffering. Her words and prayers are filled with the hope and healing she has experienced, and that she passionately wants each of us to receive and know in our life.

Stanton Lanier—Award-Winning Pianist and Composer,
Founder of Music to Light the World

The Pit of Despair has the potential to save lives. Lisa Jo's vulnerable story combined with a pathway through the twelve steps will make any addict feel less alone and capable of creating change in their own lives. Addiction is a powerful and stigmatized disease, yet Lisa Jo experiences the power of recovery and makes it accessible for all who are nervous and scared to take the first steps toward freedom.

Amy Lyden-Cardinal, MSW, CPFS

The Pit of Despair

*How GOD, PRAYER and the
12 STEPS Saved My Life from
ADDICTION*

LISA JO BARR

NASHVILLE

NEW YORK • LONDON • MELBOURNE • VANCOUVER

The Pit of Despair

How GOD, PRAYER and the 12 STEPS Saved My Life from ADDICTION

Published in New York, New York, by Morgan James Publishing. Morgan James is a trademark of Morgan James, LLC. www.MorganJamesPublishing.com

Scripture taken from the NEW AMERICAN STANDARD BIBLE®, Copyright © 1960, 1962, 1963, 1968, 1971, 1972, 1973, 1975, 1977, 1995 by The Lockman Foundation. Used by permission.

Scripture quotations marked (NLT) are taken from the Holy Bible, New Living Translation, copyright ©1996, 2004, 2015 by Tyndale House Foundation. Used by permission of Tyndale House Publishers, Carol Stream, Illinois 60188. All rights reserved.

Scripture quotations marked TPT are from The Passion Translation®. Copyright © 2017, 2018, 2020 by Passion & Fire Ministries, Inc. Used by permission. All rights reserved. ThePassionTranslation.com.

Proudly distributed by Publishers Group West®

A FREE ebook edition is available for you or a friend with the purchase of this print book.

CLEARLY SIGN YOUR NAME ABOVE

Instructions to claim your free ebook edition:
1. Visit MorganJamesBOGO.com
2. Sign your name CLEARLY in the space above
3. Complete the form and submit a photo of this entire page
4. You or your friend can download the ebook to your preferred device

ISBN 9781636983127 paperback
ISBN 9781636983134 ebook
Library of Congress Control Number:
2023944712

Cover and Interior Design by:
Chris Treccani
www.3dogcreative.net

Morgan James is a proud partner of Habitat for Humanity Peninsula and Greater Williamsburg. Partners in building since 2006.

Get involved today! Visit: www.morgan-james-publishing.com/giving-back

Call upon Me in the day of
trouble;
I shall rescue you, and you will
Honor Me.
Psalm 50:15 (NASB)

This book is dedicated to Elizabeth G.
Thanks for sharing your experience, strength and hope with me so freely, for teaching me that "We don't shoot our wounded."

You've made me a better person.

I am passing the torch and being there for other women, sponsoring
In the same ways you have been there for me.
Thanks for making this world a better place.
I love you.

More shoutouts to:
Jesus for pouring His Grace all over me and saturating me with His Love.

Robert Slayton, my mentor. Thank you for believing in me. You have shown me persistence, time management and accountability on this book project and beyond. You have also taught me grace, respect, self-compassion and acceptance. You are a great man of God, an extraordinary human being,

Also, a big thank you to the following:
Al P., John K., Stacie A, Minda I., Jeff B., Ann G., Joe G., Pammy G., Amy L., Dean D., Justin B., Brandi R., Dianna B., Marilyn S., Jenny M., Jakisha B., Todd R., Phil R., Carrie H., Nicole J., Joy G., Barbara Jean H., Robin K., Dustin S., Angela B., Renee P., Brent D., Terry W., Dylan H., Lucy V., Bob Goff, Pastor Pat, Rihanna, Isabel Allende, Leonard Cohen and Bono.

Last but not least, a gigantic thank you to my beautiful editor, Rachel Grilliot. Thank you for making my writing shine like a diamond.

God bless you all.

Contents

Prayers I've written from my heart to yours:		*xv*
Introduction		*xvii*
How to Use this Book		*xviii*

Chapter 1:	Powerlessness	1
	Writing My Story Prayer	4
	Powerlessness	5
Chapter 2:	Admitting Powerlessness (Step 1)	15
	Blessed with Connection Prayer	18
	Dial the Phone Prayer	20
	Admitting Powerlessness Prayer	24
	Rigorous Honesty Prayer	28
	Working Step One	30
	Blessing a Sponsor Prayer	33
Chapter 3:	Hope in the Hills and Valleys (Step 2)	35
	God's Hope Prayer	40
	A Step of Hope	42
	Going to a Meeting Prayer	43
Chapter 4:	Surrendering to God (Step 3)	45
	Life on Life's Terms Prayer	47
	Raise the White Flag Prayer	50
Chapter 5:	How Not to Work the Fourth Step	55
	Half Measures Availed Us Nothing Prayer	57
	The Dark Adventures of a Snow Bunny	59
	Back from Relapse Prayer	68
Chapter 6:	House Cleaning (Step 4)	73

	Releasing Resistance and Rebellion Prayer	77
	Untying the Knots of Resentment Prayer	79
	Fear Inventory Prayer	83
Chapter 7:	A Thorough Confession (Step 5)	87
	The Gift of Confessions Prayer	88
Chapter 8:	Humility and Willingness to Surrender Our Wrongs (Steps 6 and 7)	95
	Make Me Ready Prayer	97
	Humility to Let Go and Let God Prayer	103
Chapter 9:	Making Wrongs Right (Steps 8 and 9)	107
	Willingness to Make Amends Prayer	109
	Making Amends	111
	Helpless, Hopeless Confusion	112
	Taking Responsibility Prayer	116
Chapter 10:	Keeping Our Side of the Street Clean (Step 10)	119
	The Discipline of Spiritual House Cleaning Prayer	120
	Spot Checks	123
	Nightly Inventories	125
	Creating Your Own Tenth Step Nightly Inventory Sheet	125
Chapter 11:	Conscious Contact with God (Step 11)	131
	The Magnificence of Meditation	132
	Being Present With Yourself and With God	134
	Conscious Contact With God Prayer	136
	The Power of Prayer	138
	Two-Way Prayer	140
Chapter 12:	Service as A Way of Life (Step 12)	145
	Being of Service Prayer	148
Chapter 13:	How to Write your Own Prayers	151
	Word Sculpting	155
Chapter 14:	More 12-step Inspired Prayers	159
	Sweet Sleep and Gratitude Prayer	159
	Healing Spiraling Shame Prayer	162

Anxiety and Depression Prayer 164
Stay in Today Prayer 167
Tools of The Program Prayer 169
Lead me to Serenity Prayer 171
Faith Without Works is Dead Prayer 172
Chapter 15: Food Addiction 175
Powerlessness: A Step One Issue 175
My Food Story 177
Sugar as Heroin 177
My Father's Restaurant Peace Pipe 181
A Life-Threatening Addiction 181
Fast Forward 182
Consequences of Powerlessness Over the Disease
of Food Addiction 184
Shout Out for Your Help 188

References 191
Prayers I've written from my heart to yours: 193
About the Author 195

Prayers I've written from my heart to yours:

Writing my Story Prayer	4
Blessed with Connection Prayer	18
Dial the Phone Prayer	20
Admitting Powerlessness Prayer	24
Rigorous Honesty Prayer	28
Blessing a Sponsor Prayer	33
God's Hope Prayer	40
Going to a Meeting Prayer	43
Life on Life's Terms Prayer	47
Raise the White Flag Prayer	50
Half Measures Availed Us Nothing Prayer	57
Back From Relapse Prayer	68
Releasing Resistance and Rebellion Prayer	77
Untying the Knots of Resentment Prayer	79
Fear Inventory Prayer	83
The Gifts of Confession Prayer	88
Make Me Ready Prayer	97
Humility to Let Go and Let God Prayer	103
Willingness to Make Amends Prayer	109
Taking Responsibility Prayer	116
The Discipline of Spiritual House Cleaning Prayer	120
Conscious Contact with God Prayer	136
Being of Service Prayer	148
Sweet Sleep and Gratitude Prayer	159
Healing Spiraling Shame Prayer	162
Anxiety and Depression Prayer	164

Stay in Today Prayer   167
Tools of the Program Prayer   169
Lead me to Serenity Prayer   171
Faith Without Works is Dead Prayer   172

Introduction

I lay face down in the mud. I was dragged all over town, day and night, until I passed out. I'd swear, just before losing consciousness, to never do it again. Ever. Then the following day I would find myself face down in the mud again, swirling in the vicious cycle of addiction and shame, endlessly repeating itself. Spiritually bankrupt, the only thing that mattered in my life was getting high. There was no room for anything else.

This is not only part of my story but is the bleak reality for millions of suffering addicts from all over the world. The drug of choice doesn't matter. It could be drugs, alcohol, sex, gambling, work, shopping, food or video games. You name it. A global epidemic, addiction is a behavior or consumption that is used over and over again by a person to numb out or escape discomfort, even when the consequences are harmful and all consuming.

No matter how dark and disconnected an addict's life becomes, some are given the gift of desperation. For these addicts things get so bad, they hit a bottom and decide they cannot continue living the insanity of active addiction. Their first prayer is, "God, help me." There is hope for those reaching out to God with prayer. In my journey, hope and redemption came in the form of a design for living that includes connecting with God and other recovering addicts by working the 12-step program.

Around the clock, thousands upon thousands of recovering addicts meet together anonymously in 12-step meetings, going around the room sharing their stories, feelings, experience, strength and hope. They open and close the meetings with The Serenity Prayer.

Addicts, who were once spiritually bankrupt, learn how to rely on God. They begin to take responsibility for their lives and to know they cannot operate successfully on self-will alone. The greatest spiritual experience in an addict's life is to discover, develop and deepen a relationship with God. This comes from talking to God through a process known as prayer.

I attended my first 12-step meeting in 2007, placing a dangerous life-threatening addiction to sex and cocaine into recovery. I have experienced a cornucopia of addictions--to cigarettes, food, sex, "love," and cocaine. By the grace of His Holiness, through my ever-growing conscious communication and relationship to God, meditation, therapy, and working the 12-step program, I have experienced a deep healing and continue to live a happy, fulfilling and purpose-filled life, one day at a time.

My experience, strength and hope is weaved throughout this book along with prayers I've written. You are cordially invited to participate. The prayers are presented in both singular and plural forms so that you can say them alone or together out loud with friends, family or fellows in the program.

Many folks who are addicted don't know what to say to God because they have lived in isolation and disconnection for so long. Mark Dejesus, author of *The Heart Healing Journey*, writes that one reason we don't pray is because we don't know what to say to God. This book will help you get comfortable speaking to God through the conversational tone and ease of these prayers. They are steeped in the familiarity of the 12-step language and speak to God as if we have a living, friendly and warm relationship with Him; something we can all attain if we keep praying and listening.

I have a chapter giving you tips and suggestions on how to write your own powerful customized prayers, to find your own words to praise and thank God.

The purpose of this book is to inspire you to talk to God in order to deepen your trust and faith in Him and to jumpstart your prayer life in order to live a quality of recovery beyond your wildest dreams.

How to Use this Book

In the table of contents and in the index at the back of the book, you can find a list of all the different prayers I've written along with their page numbers and what they are about. I've written prayers related to the steps, tools and ideas that are related to the 12-step program. The prayers come from my heart.

Pray by Yourself or Pray with Others

The prayers are in the "I" version, or singular, so you can say them out loud by yourself and are also written in the "we" version, or plural, so that you can pray them together with another person or as a group.

Toward the end of the book is a chapter on how to write your own prayers. I give you my insight and my experience on my process and how you can write your own powerful prayers, plus examples.

IMPORTANT DISCLAIMER: I am not an **authority** speaking on behalf of any 12-step fellowship, or on how the steps "should" be worked. Steps and the personal experience of doing so are as unique to the individual. Kind of like snowflakes. Each person experiences their recovery journey differently. We all have our own individual experience.

My book is humbly my experience through the horrors of active addiction to the healing and redemption of my soul through my relationship with Christ. This is merely my experience, strength and hope along with my journey with Christ.

Chapter 1:

Powerlessness

O our God, will You not judge them? For we are powerless
before this great multitude who are coming against us; nor
do we know what to do, but our eyes are on You.
2 Chronicles 20:12 (NASB)

Addiction infiltrated my soul and held my sexuality hostage. It corrupted and confused me, and without Christ's salvation, I would not have been able to get out of the tangled web alive. The disease had me suspended and stuck in a rut of doing the same thing over and over, expecting a different result. God was always present even though I had shut the door on His Ever-Loving Presence that later gave me the power to forgive, move past hurting myself, and see and treat myself as the child of the Most High God that I truly am.

Nobody becomes an addict on purpose. I didn't hurt myself deliberately. Addiction is a disease. I did not wake up one day, and, just for kicks, decide to flush my life down the toilet time and again. I did not just make progress in recovery, only to relapse–to go back in the river of filth, drowning in a gutter, starving spiritually. I was not a bad person, nor was I weak. As a matter of fact, us addicts are some of the strongest people I know on the planet and certainly the most focused. After all, for decades, we only had one thing to live for with a razor-sharp focus: our drug of choice.

In my life, I became addicted to substances and behavior. I was addicted to sex, cocaine, cigarettes, "love" addiction (or infatuation/obsession with men) and compulsive overeating. No matter what addiction was active at a given time, it was always pure hell 24/7. If I was using, then I was suffering.

All addiction is self-medication. I used these substances and behaviors as numbing agents, an escape from tremendous emotional pain and from feeling any discomfort whatsoever. At the extreme, I even used drugs as an alternative to killing myself, when I had reached rock bottom with my mental health. I used addiction to mask severe depression that was a symptom of the chemical imbalance of Bipolar I and the horrendous emotional flashbacks of Complex PTSD. The more overwhelmed or depressed I got, the more I increased the dose of my drugs in order to get the same effect. At the same time, I found myself chasing after a higher high.

The disease of addiction was progressive. When you go back to using after a period of sobriety, the disease merely picks up where it left off and quickly gets worse. It's as though it's in the parking lot doing push ups, lurking and waiting for me to rest on my laurels, drawing me back to slipping and falling into this horrendous lifestyle of active addiction once again.

I believed in God for a couple decades, but never felt close to Him until I was at a Buddhist Temple in Bangkok at the age of 25. I was waiting 3 hours for my train to depart to Chiang Mai up north. With luggage in hand, I took a taxi to the first Buddhist temple I could find. I loved the big gold Buddhas, their tranquil expressions, the smell of incense and the peaceful solitude away from the whizzing traffic. There was a sheltered open-air temple that drew me in. I was standing outside and staring into the brightly lit temple, with hundreds of candle flames dancing and big pillowy clouds of incense rising to the sky.

No one was around except stray dogs that had sores all over their bodies. All of a sudden, I heard a clear still voice say to me, "Dearest child, I have been here all along. You have never been alone. I've been by your side ever since you were born."

I instantly knew who it was. It was God. I started crying and crying, buckled over with overwhelming joy.

The stress of loneliness left every cell of my body just then, for a moment that felt like an eternity. It was as if all of me knew that God will always be with me, even if I turn my back from Him. My loneliness vanished for a long period. This shift and the warm awareness that God was with me, made me cry so hard that tears were streaming down my face, hitting the pavement. I cried so much that I could barely catch my breath. What I experienced was a miracle of God's Love.

God went on to speak to me as I sat down on a concrete step, "I want you to get out of all of those groups you are in."

And I did.

What God was referring to was the two metaphysical cults I belonged to. I went to their meetings and read their books, performed "magic" which was basically getting lost in smoking mirrors. I tried to make things happen on self-will alone. I thought that I could change life on life's terms. I studied all the metaphysics that I could get my hands on, looking and searching for something bigger than myself, searching for God, but not knowing His name. I did not find Him there. Dabbling in metaphysical muck put me in a lot of danger–physically, mentally, spiritually, emotionally. It definitely dysregulated me emotionally.

When I got home from my Thai trip, I sold all my witchcraft and occult books. I watched one of these group members haul a bunch of my books away in a shopping cart down the sidewalk. I stood there and the darkness left me.

Cults are dangerous groups disguised as light. They are shrouded in deception and manipulative darkness. Places full of people idolizing themselves or others. These people were trying so hard to play God. They worshiped false idols, worshiped themselves at times and worshiped others. Even as some of the cult members threatened me for leaving, God covered me in His light and protection. God was with me all along and turned it all around for me.

I was not raised in any religion. My father, who grew up Jewish, was a narcissistic agnostic who constantly made fun of religious people. He was suspicious of them and did not allow my mom, who was Southern Baptist, to take us to church. So, I grew to fear religion and went around as an angry teen saying that "religion leaves a bad taste in my mouth."

Looking back though, Christ was with me and spoke to me gently and firmly on my Thai trip. God took my hand and cradled me in His Love. For a moment, I felt at ease. The war was over. I was a soldier that had been fighting for so long. My Creator's everlasting, unconditional love felt so right, whole, complete.

Whenever I relapsed, the dire consequences surfaced and the more sick I became. Active addiction always gave me amnesia. It made me forget all about God being there by my side. I had taken God off the throne and was worshiping the false idols of addictive substances and compulsive behaviors instead. God had not moved. I had moved. But it was He who redeemed me, saved me from the madness through working the 12 steps.

My story is not an easy one to tell, so I wrote a prayer that I said before I sat down to write this book. It helped anchor me and grow my faith that I could do it.

Writing My Story Prayer

God,

    Grant me the endurance and the strength to write. Show me Your Power moving through me, with the gift of writing that You gave me so generously.

    Let the words come to me. Let the organization fall into place. This book—my work of art, branded by my creativity, my personality, my journey. This testimony is our Masterpiece, God, with Your Divine Guidance working through me, in safety and enjoyment, with pen and paper and fingers tapping on keyboards. My feelings are not facts, yet they are used as paint to express my emotional stories captured in words. Guide me, Jesus, from tripping over my past. Propel me to glide into the present.

Let me act on the courage to write a word. A sentence. A paragraph. A chapter. A book.

Help me. Dear Lord, to bring writing into more of my time—into my life more vividly and regularly. God, help me to sink deeper into my true love of putting words down on paper. Reconnect me with the powerful tools of language and story. I feel the courage in my heart to explore and express Your Glory in the pages of this book.

Keep me safe from scary memories, Heavenly Father.

Guide me to do Your Will.

In Jesus's Name I pray.

Amen

Powerlessness

My innocence was lost when I was molested as a child by an uncle who babysat me while my parents went to a Neil Diamond concert.

When I was 13, my rageaholic father called me a whore and accused me of doing drugs. I hadn't picked up anything yet and I was still a virgin. In high school, when the drugs were offered to me, I figured that my dad already thought I did it, so why not. When sex presented itself, I also felt this caved-in defeat right at my heart, so I didn't fight the invitation. I used sex as a substitute for love. I needed to be needed.

I started having sex at age 14 with much older guys. Sex seemed, from the very beginning, to be insatiable, yet "manageable" at first. It was a progressive disease.

I met Mark one hot summer night on a dancefloor at an all-age night-club called After the Fox. The song "Into the Groove" by Madonna came on and my friends and I all ran up at once to move to this catchy new song. From across the dance floor, I felt his eyes gazing upon me. Mark was a tall, dark and handsome man. He danced beautifully to the music. He made his way through the crowd, all while looking me in the eyes. Without saying a word, his hands entwined with mine and we moved together, in perfect sync. I had never felt so high from a mere touch of the hand. He smelled good too as he held me tight on the dancefloor, tighter as the song ended. He introduced himself.

He was a 19-year-old and still lived with his parents. During our telephone calls, I told him all about the violence and emotional abuse I continued to endure from my father. He offered to help me run away from home.

So I did.

The night before, I put pen to paper. I knew if this journey I was about to embark on didn't work, I'd have to kill myself. I was not coming back here. I had an uneasiness that it was going to be near to impossible to run away from my father. He had a way of manipulating, getting information out of my friends and hunting me down. So I wrote a suicide note expressing all my hurt and that I was desperate to leave the violence behind even if it meant ending my life.

That morning I met Mark and he helped me move some stuff out of my house, including the Fender electric guitar my father had given me after not learning how to play it himself. I wanted to bring all the music with me. It was my only salvation at the time. The only thing that made me feel safe. Music. I had the album *War* by U2 memorized and it got me through many nights of fighting like a soldier. It gave me strength. When nobody was home, I'd blast it and sing along to every word. Siouxsie and the Banshees also became part of my soundtrack to that era. Memorizing every song as I pedaled away on a stationary bike in my parent's basement, blasting music when they weren't home. Singing and yelling the lyrics.

After moving my stereo into a friend's house, up three flights of stairs, Mark drove us across town, listening to "Voices Carry" on the radio. I told him to turn it up to drown out my thoughts. I was very anxious about this whole thing. He snuck me into his parents house before they came home from work. Mark and his father went to McDonald's while I lay on his floor on the other side of his bed, away from his door, listening to his mother washing dishes. He brought me French fries half an hour later. That night, I slept in his bed. When we kissed for the first time, it was like I was free falling down an elevator shaft. I was instantly in love. I had never felt that before.

Within a few months, we were having sex. The more we had it, the harder I fell in love with him. I confused sex with love from the very beginning. All I wanted was to be loved.

I became obsessed with Mark. I put him on a pedestal where he could do no wrong. I called him constantly, desperate to reach him. When I did, we would talk and I'd fill up with being wanted. As soon as we hung up, the emptiness would come flooding back. I couldn't get him off my mind. There were many times I showed up at his home and his work uninvited. I just couldn't stop thinking about him, couldn't get enough. He sizzled in my mind day in and day out, all the time. It was as if all I had to live for was his attention. I couldn't live without his affection, our sex. Negative attention was still attention, and I needed attention from a man. I had to have him prove his "love" for me. I lied to him in order to stay in his life, even when things went sour. I told him I was pregnant and he gave me $150 to get an abortion. That money was proof that he still cared.

He cheated on his girlfriends with me. I didn't care. I just needed more of him. I would go to any lengths to be with him; stoop to any level. It was as if my life depended on it. I lived and breathed for this man. I was so desperate. So sad, even suicidal. So uncomfortable and full of anxiety and turmoil that I was empty inside.

Mark and I were lovers, off and on, for a few years. Hurting each other emotionally and compulsively every time we spent time together. He told me he loved me as a way to manipulate me to do things for him. I just turned 15 years old. I didn't want to do the things he wanted me to do, but I did anything for him. I thought that by doing what he asked, I'd sustain our love. I was lost without him. Like a blind woman covered in dust walking in an unfamiliar city all alone. I needed his love, his guidance, his comfort.

One time, out of jealous rage, I orchestrated my friends to vandalize his car, which was parked at the all-age nightclub. I was stuck at home that night so over the phone, I told my best friend to pour a large Wendy's Frosty onto his windshield. And she did.

Mark eventually told me to stop calling him. He had had enough. But I could not stop. He was always on my mind. I kept calling him, desperate to hear his voice. The phone just rang and rang.

On Valentine's Day I showed up at his work. I confessed my love to him. When he told me to leave him alone, he went to the back through the doors that said "employees only." I followed him into the kitchen. He yelled for help and pushed me hard backward, telling me to get out. His boss showed up, 86'ed me and told me I could never step foot in his establishment again.

Love addiction causes a person to hallucinate love even when it's not there. It doesn't care about other people's space or boundaries. I always invaded the space of the person I was obsessed with. It felt like I didn't have a choice to act this way. I was a sick young woman.

At age 17, I began sleeping around. I had more frequent sex, sometimes on consecutive nights with different partners. My relationships with men were intense and short lived. There was always a lot of drama. I was on a rollercoaster emotionally, medicating my undiagnosed bipolar with compulsive sex and "love" addiction. I tried to ease the excruciating pain I was in from living in a war zone as a child and teen. I was the main target of my father's rage.

One of my boyfriends, Thomas, broke up with me. I met him on the dance floor, too. I continued to obsess over him, living in a fantasy that he missed me and would soon be back. When I saw him at a local concert, with a new girlfriend, I made a public scene. I had a hard time controlling my anger.

Another lover, Derrick, whom I lived with for a while in another state, agreed to have an open relationship. I pretended to be his main squeeze. He was a great kisser and I had met him a couple weeks earlier one New Year's Eve, while on ecstasy. Immediately after having sex, I fell in love. I went back home, gave away all my belongings and drove back to be with him two weeks later. I was 20 years old. I began sleeping with our roommate. There was nothing wrong with being promiscuous. After all, we had an open relationship. That was our agreement. However, when the tables turned, and I discovered my "boyfriend" was sleeping with another woman, I went into a jealous rage. I suffered greatly in the fresh dew the summer morning after discovering his "betrayal." I worked the graveyard shift and rode my bicycle home every night, before the sun came up. I went to climb into bed with Derrick only to discover a naked woman sleeping next to him. She had literally taken my place. I ran outside, stood in the wet soil, right when the sun was coming up, and cried my guts out, feeling the rawness of rejection and abandonment. All my wounds ripped wide open.

One evening, in the middle of the night, I was boiling mad thinking about Derrick in our old room with his new lover. My old room I had shared with him was right below me. The whole house was asleep. I took a hammer and nails and began pounding them into the wood in my new attic room, into my floor which was his ceiling, with all my rage behind it, disturbing Derrick's sleep and causing him to feel unsafe in his own home.

Even though I was in a state of perpetually craving more sexual encounters, I was also desperately craving intimacy. I didn't know what a healthy relationship with a man even looked like. It was not patterned for me at home growing up. I had no conscious relationship with my Heavenly Father either. God was there but He was not on my radar yet.

The deeper I got into addiction, the more my friendships were strained. I wasn't present. I was obsessed with sex and romantic intrigue around the clock. I canceled plans with friends in order to be with the object of my lust or "love." My entire life was a secret and I had nobody to talk to about it. I was sick with secrets that isolated me from the rest of the world.

I spent hours and hours in fantasy. I wasted precious time doing nothing but getting lost in a labyrinth of daydreaming, chasing my own tail and spinning out of control.

The addiction drew me to emotionally unavailable men. The only thing that comforted me was to have sex with more strangers. I'd fall "in love" with some of these nameless faces. If they showed me a gesture of tenderness, I clinched onto it, desperate for attention, for acceptance, for love. I had not given my life to Christ at this point. I didn't know that all of these things could be filled up with God's unconditional love. That it could empower me to do great things.

I began to travel extensively after getting a job with an airline. It was a lifelong dream to see and experience different cultures around the world. I was 24 years old. In a foreign country, I felt the freedom to be whoever I wanted to be. While in Bali, I had a whirlwind romance. I almost married a local man after only knowing him for 2 days.

All over Asia, I would have sex in silent dark rooms with men who did not speak English. On these trips, while acting out, I felt so alive when I was with a lover. Empty, lonely and depressed when I wasn't.

I experienced severe depression while in Hong Kong. I was walking around the city, crying while walking to catch the ferry to Hong Kong island, crying at the Waterford and in museums. I learned quickly during this trip that acting out sexually made my depression go away. It obliterated it. Then afterward, things would come crashing down hard. So, I acted out more frequently.

I had sex in Kowloon Park late at night, climbing high fences and gates with a man from England to get inside an otherwise locked up park. By doing so, I risked my safety, I could have been thrown in jail. Powerlessness.

On a work project in India, I had an affair with a man who worked for the outsourcing company we were doing business with. We would kiss passionately in the elevator during our shift before it opened. I risked losing my precious job. More powerlessness.

In 2000, I married a sexually compulsive alcoholic. The sex was so good that I could not resist saying yes to his proposal. Again, I confused sex for love.

During my four-year marriage, I robbed myself of time, gas money and emotional well-being by stalking my husband late at night in downtown Denver, trying to hunt him down at bars, suspicious of him cheating and attempting to control his drinking.

Every month, my husband and I would rack up $200-$300 cable bills for access to adult programming. It was like a scary numbing agent. It felt unsafe but it was intense enough to drown out the noise in my head. At least for a second. Then, it would all come crashing down.

After leaving my husband and getting a divorce, I didn't have sex for a full year. In late 2005, I placed my first online hook-up ad. I met up with Jacob at a Barnes and Noble bookstore. We sized each other up and we both liked what we saw. We went into the quiet bookstore looking for an empty aisle. He kissed me. I was on fire and that was the beginning of having intense encounters with strange men using the internet. I could set aside my emotions and get sex anytime I wanted. I was in "control." I was hooked.

My company moved me to Chicago in 2006, where I did not know a single person. I was put up in a nice hotel for a few weeks, while I looked for an apartment to settle into. While living at the Marriott, I posted more ads on craigslist. First, it was a three-times-a-week habit. It quickly turned into an every night encounter. I was meeting these men in the hotel bar before inviting them up to my room.

I discovered new hookup sites. Once priding myself for staying away from married men, I started sleeping with them, with an inflated ego.

I sought out rough experiences. The fear and intensity brought me into new heights. Once, I was physically injured by a stranger. This did not stop me or slow me down.

I loved my job with the airlines, but I put it in jeopardy. I had FMLA (Family Medical Leave Act) for bipolar and complex PTSD in the form of panic attacks at the office. I'd call in sick, chronically, and act out sexually.

I was so depressed that I'd stay in bed for 3 days straight–not bathing and forcing myself to sleep as much as possible. The only thing that got me out of bed was the prospect of a new sexual encounter. One day, on my way to work, I called in sick and rented a hotel room down the street. I scheduled men like they were appointments. This was the beginning of acting out several times a day with different men.

I eventually got a demotion at work for missing so much time. The position I lost was a position I loved. My supervisor had to present evidence against me at humiliating union proceedings. The company won. I lost.

I stopped being involved at work. I always loved to go the extra mile, taking great pride in the company and being on special committees to better the work environment. I had no extra energy to do anything but my addiction. It had taken over.

I sought after emotionally abusive encounters; new forms of perversion, of darkness. More intensity. More danger. Sex and BDSM became like heroin. I was letting strangers restrain and take advantage of me. Then doing whatever they wanted, even when this included violence and emotional abuse. At the time, I did not see this as dangerous at all. It was just another way to desperately quench my sexual hunger. I was in extreme denial.

I engaged with police officers who liked to dominate women.

I began to get into group sex. At this point, I honestly wanted to become a sex slave for the rest of my life and started looking and hunting to make this a reality. God suddenly stepped in and did not let this happen. He loved me too much.

I would stay out until 3 or 4 a.m. on a regular basis, which was hard on my body and destabilized me emotionally.

There was one partner that I "fell in love with." When we abruptly stopped sleeping together, we still hung out as friends. I discovered he smoked a lot of pot. He was a few years older than me and his name was Gary. I crossed my own boundary of being clean from drugs for over a decade, I started smoking marijuana around the clock with him. I did it because I thought that to spend time with him, I needed to do what he liked to do. Soon, the highs took over. We would smoke an exorbitant amount of pot and Gary would turn to me and ask, "You good, hun?"

I would lie to him even though I was high as a kite and tell him I didn't feel much, so he would give me more. There was no ceiling on me doing drugs again. I could not stop. Pot was a gateway to harder substances.

I was obsessed with Gary and after he wanted me to stop calling him every day, I would start showing up at his house, unannounced. One time, I stalked him by parking my car in front of his house late at night.

I started using pornography between acting out. Empty, fake images of abuse and objectification. I lost track of time when using pornography and this caused me to be chronically late for work. My whole life revolved around sex. Watching it. Hunting for it. Chasing it. Doing it.

Sex addiction was lonely, desperate, cunning and baffling.

Without a conscious relationship with God and the 12-step program, I would be dead by now.

Chapter 2:

Admitting Powerlessness (Step 1)

*For while we were still helpless, at
The right time Christ died for the ungodly.*
Romans 5:6 (NASB)

O ne dismal morning, I woke up with ideas and schemes of how to feed the addiction, how to get my fix for the day, where to look. I laid there in bed longer than usual. When I closed my eyes, I saw a big yellow sign.

Behind my eyes it read "Sex Addicts Anonymous 7 p.m." I could have sworn this was a memory I had of when I lived in Downtown Denver and it was at some church on 14th Ave. that I had passed while driving and turned to a friend saying, "Sex addict? Who would want to be that?!"

But why would an anonymous group be so public about their meeting information? I still don't know if this memory was real or not. It didn't really matter. What mattered is that I saw the sign. And I pursued its message.

I opened up my laptop and typed the words "Sex Addicts Anonymous" into Google. The site came up and then I got another inspiring idea. I was going to attend one of their meetings. I looked them up and picked one of them. I wrote down the details on a small piece of paper. It stayed in my coat pocket for three and a half weeks. Every time I put my hands in my pockets and felt that little piece of paper, I was reminded of my plan to go to one of these meetings. I was confused and somewhat terrified of what I might find. God was about to give me the gift of what I feared the most—intimacy. In this case, it was in the form of companionship with others in the program along the road to recovery.

I finally mustered up the courage to go. I remember breathing heavily as I stood outside on the sidewalk, looking up at the church where the meeting was held. It was almost 7 p.m. I looked at the piece of paper that was in my pocket. The numbers matched the ones on the church. Yep, this was it.

I went inside, walked up the stairs and took a sharp left into what reminded me of a big living room. It had beautiful couches, tables and lamps all around, carpet and warmth from the cold outside. I was sweating profusely and shaking. I could barely breathe. I asked someone if this was the sex addicts anonymous meeting. He said, "You're in the right place."

He pointed me to an empty metal fold-out chair; told me to have a seat. I was really scared as I looked around the room. I counted; there were 30 men and me. No other women. The room was full of laughter and friendly comradery. Most of the men were dressed up as if they had prominent jobs in the community. I didn't know for sure, though. The laughter died down and the meeting started. They said the Serenity Prayer together:

> God,
> Grant me the serenity
> To accept the things I cannot change,
> Courage to change the things I can,

And the wisdom to know the difference.
Amen

There were announcements and then these men took turns reading from a book that was passed around the room. I had no idea what that reading was about because I couldn't concentrate. I was way too nervous. I stared into space. The air had a sense of safety about it. I began to let my guard down and slipped out of my jacket. Then, it was time for people to start sharing. I paid more attention. The man who ran the meeting said that we could share on the reading, on our experience, strength and hope, or whatever was on our heart.

A man across from me "got current" sharing his personal experience. His words had meaning to me. We spoke the same language. I could relate so much to him and his struggles; it was as if he were telling my story. His story reached me and embraced me from across the room. The details were exactly like mine. I breathed a sigh of relief. Up until that point, I thought that I was the only human being in the world acting the way I did; that I was truly alone in my experiences as a sex addict. I felt so much shame. Suddenly, now, I had a blanket of tranquility wrapped around me in this house of God. Here sat my brothers who all accepted me and began to love me the more meetings I attended and the more they got to know me. I was not alone, and I had found my people. I kept whispering to myself, "I have found my people."

After that first meeting, a few of the men came up to me and introduced themselves and wanted to know if I wanted their phone numbers in case I wanted to talk to someone. I took their numbers–little lifelines on tiny pieces of paper that had handwritten telephone numbers and names on them. These became lifesavers during points of my recovery. Men who I once objectified. Real people with real lives and names and faces. People who struggled in the same way I did, but were full of life and laughter. Life rafts.

How did I connect with others when I felt so alone for so long in the addiction? How did I even begin to trust anyone when I had not trusted myself for so long? It was only by God's Grace. It was through faith that others could help me, relate to me and accept me.

So many friendly faces warmly invited me to contact them at any time. How did I pick up that 300-pound phone and connect with another human being when I was not doing well, when I was in withdrawal, vulnerable, hurting and not perfect? When I still wanted to act on addiction to feel connected and to fill up that empty feeling inside?

I felt the fear, took that positive risk to act as if others could help me and took the leap to make the calls. I acted as if I was not alone, even though the disease told me I was. I acted despite my fear. Thus began the friendships I had not even known were possible. God showed me that I was not alone.

In my disease I was isolated, and my life was full of unspoken secrets. This created fertile ground for the addiction to reach new lows. I wouldn't dare reach out for help. I had too much shame to admit to anyone what was going on. My silence was driven by a delusion that I could help myself by my own will. "Self-sufficiency" when I actually needed help. I spent days without speaking to anyone I knew personally. My drug of choice gave an illusion that everyone was my friend, giving me a false sense of the intimacy that I craved. All I met were other sick people like me. Around my new 12-step friends I felt the warmth, safety and friendliness of others that gave me a peace and connection I have never known. They shook my hands and gave me loving hugs. I breathed a sigh of relief knowing I was not alone. There were others who struggled like I had. By the grace of God, in the light of recovery, these new loving faces, other recovering addicts, became my friends.

***

Blessed with Connection Prayer

Dear God,

Bless me with companions as I trudge the road of happy destiny. Bless me with genuine friendships where I feel completely comfortable being myself. In the spirit of Your Divine Generosity, shower my days with laughter, with shared stories, with great conversations, with shoulders to cry on and smiling faces to celebrate with. Surround me with supportive people who understand me. Grow and expand my kind and caring tribe. Cradle me in platonic love where The Holy Spirit moves through the people around me. Provide me with safety and warmth. Let isolation be behind me. Connect me with others who are diligently working their program, who all want to be in conscious contact with You, Lord. Open my mind to learn from others. Bless me with comradery as I learn from the experience, strength and hope from others.

In Christ's Name I pray.

Amen

* * *

Dear God,

Bless us with companions as we trudge the road of happy destiny. Bless us with genuine friendship where we feel completely comfortable being ourselves. In the spirit of Your Divine Generosity, shower our days with laughter, with shared stories, with great conversations, with shoulders to cry on and smiling faces to celebrate with. Surround us with supportive people who understand us. Grow and expand our kind and caring tribe. Cradle us in platonic love where The Holy Spirit moves through the people around us. Provide us with safety and warmth. Let isolation be behind us. Connect us with others who are diligently working their program, who all want to be in conscious contact with You, Lord. Open our minds to learn from others. Bless us with comradery as we learn from the experience, strength and hope from others.

In Christ's Name we pray.

Amen

The meeting outside the meeting involved fellowship at local cafes with exchanged phone numbers and invitations to reach out when I was struggling. It was a challenge to pick up the phone and dial. I didn't want to bother anyone. I half thought that I didn't deserve the help and was determined to "go it alone."

I tried that a million times and it didn't work. I just got lost in my head and lost in my life. I could not do this alone. It was too much for one person to endure or to figure out. God and others were needed as part of the solution. I took that risk and finally felt the fear and made a call, waiting nervously while the phone rang. A warm voice of one of the guys from my home group answered and genuinely cared, asking me how my recovery was going. We talked about it. I was able to share in real time, where I was at. It felt like a relief. My friend on the phone gave me his experience and encouragement. That's when I knew there was something special about using the phone to call others in the program.

Dial the Phone Prayer

God,

Show me that I am not alone, even when I feel like I am. Make my phone lighter, so that I may pick it up and dial the numbers of my fellows. Help me use it as a way of bringing me out of isolation.

Thank You for giving me protection in the storm, for keeping me out of harm's way. Release me from the grip of any anxiety and resistance to reach out. Help me make sound and healthy decisions, despite the cravings.

Thank You for clarity after the chaos, for courage in the presence of fear, for love in the presence of loneliness. I praise You for matching calamity with serenity.

Thank You for finding a way even when I saw none. Guide me deeper and deeper into recovery. Help me to work the program to the best of my ability, despite fear, and to know I cannot control the addiction, that I am indeed powerless over it. I praise You for my eyes so I may see clearly, for my ears to hear Your Truth, and for knowing that You are the one running the show.

God, take me under Your wing and bless me with freedom from despair. Grant me healthy companions along the way. Make it a pleasure to meet supportive people to talk one-on-one with over the phone. Help me program their numbers into my phone and to act on Your Inspiration to reach out and connect throughout my day.

Guide me and help me to make a call today; to reach out to a program person, to ask them how they are doing and to be present by just listening. Help me to keep my own stuff to myself during the call. Guide me to fulfill the need to be of service to this person and guide my attention to being there fully in the present moment. Help me take this one simple step to get out of my head...to make one phone call. Grant me a higher level of listening to You and my friend on the phone with all my heart and soul.

Take my hand and show me that others understand.

In the name of Jesus I pray.

Amen

* * *

God,

Show us that we are not alone, even when we feel like we are. Make our phones lighter, so that we may pick them up and dial the numbers of our fellows. Help us use them as a way of bringing us out of isolation.

Thank You for giving us protection in the storm, for keeping us out of harm's way. Release us from the grip of any anxiety and resistance to reach out. Help us make sound and healthy decisions, despite the cravings.

Thank You for clarity after the chaos, for courage in the presence of fear, for love in the presence of loneliness. We praise You for matching calamity with serenity.

Thank You for finding a way even when we saw none. Guide us deeper and deeper into recovery. Help us to work the program to the best of our ability, despite fear, and to know that we cannot control the addiction, that we are indeed powerless over it. We praise You for our eyes so we may see clearly, for our ears to hear Your Truth, and for knowing that You are the one running the show.

God, take us under Your wing and bless us with freedom from despair. Grant us healthy companions along the way. Make it a pleasure to meet supportive people to talk one-on-one with over the phone. Help us program their numbers into our phones and act on Your Inspiration to reach out and connect throughout our day.

Guide us and help us to make a call today; to reach out to a program person, to ask them how they are doing and to be present by just listening. Help us to keep our own stuff to ourselves during the call. Guide us to fulfill the need to be of service to this person and guide our attention to being there fully in the present moment. Help us take this one simple step to get out of our heads...to make one phone call. Grant us a higher level of listening to You and my friend on the phone with all our heart and soul.

Take our hands and show us that others understand.

In the name of Jesus we pray.

Amen

At the end of the meeting after saying the serenity prayer again, members of the 12-step group all said in unison, "Keep coming back! It works if you work it, and work it cuz you're worth it!"

So, I kept coming back. First, with one foot in the program and one foot out. But, I showed up once a week, and it was changing me. My self-care improved. My energy slowed down some of the time. If only for that one hour a week, I was staying sober during the time of the meeting. I would sometimes go out afterward and desperately try to get my fix again, out of habit. Or I'd go to a meeting after acting out all day. These meetings were an antidote to the helplessness and loneliness and desperation I felt as an active addict.

My acting out was never the same after attending my first 12-step meeting. In the back of my mind, I heard the stories and felt the warmth of the connections with my recovery brothers and sisters who understood. They understood that this was a sickness, too. This released the toxic shame of the accuser from my soul. My recovery brothers forgave me. They loved me while I was still in the disease and the process of learning how to love myself.

The 12-step program was confusing at first. I didn't want to release the grip that I had on using my drug of choice. There was a delusion that I could control the addiction by doing more of it. I was frightened and terrified to admit to powerlessness. I did not even like that word.

The program had to use a harsh word like "powerless" in order to grab our attention. It was no laughing matter the types of chaotic messes our entangled lives had become as a result of using our drug of choice. The word "powerless" was vivid, depressing, clear. It was like a slap in the face. Thank God that some of us woke up from the sting of that slap.

Waking up once did not guarantee sobriety. We addicts had amnesia when it came to admitting powerlessness. We kept taking our will back. Trying to arrange the scene to suit our needs. We kept trying to control reality again and again by using.

I had long abandoned God, whom I found at that Buddhist temple in Thailand years before. I was not worthy to dwell in His Love. I had lost connection with others, with myself and with Him. Even after I got some traction and began to see that God was all powerful and I was not, I had to remind myself every morning that I was powerless over the addiction–that I could not control it in any shape or form. It was an impossible and dangerous mission to keep pursuing–thinking I was all-powerful–putting my ego on the throne with the substance as my higher power.

I had shut the door on Christ. He did not abandon me. He was waiting patiently. God was always there, protecting me and working to wake me up from my stupor.

The more I moved into recovery, the more I was able to establish that all important connection with God. The power of the trinity embraced me–Jesus Christ, Heavenly Father and His Holy Spirit. It was only by the grace of God that I came out alive on the other side and I am now going to become a beacon of light for other recovering addicts, to teach them what I have learned and to live in the light of the Holy Spirit.

Admitting Powerlessness Prayer

Dear Heavenly Father,

I come to You in desperation. I keep trying to control what I cannot control. I have been bruised and battered by the addiction. After swearing never to pick up again, the next day I go back to the same miserable state of being in active addiction, trying to control my God-given feelings–numbing them, pushing them down or shutting them out.

God, please help my head and my heart see how powerless I am over addiction, that I cannot control it but rather, it controls me when I use it.

I am not God. Heavenly Father, You are God and I'm not. You are All Mighty and All Powerful, and I am not.

Guide me to work the program to the best of my ability. Grant me humility, for I know little. Make me teachable and break the chains of thinking I know it all. Help me to become part of a community that understands, that welcomes me with open arms. Let my actions reflect that I cannot control anything outside myself, including people, places and things. Let me take the action, on faith, to get a sponsor who will help me to navigate the program that was created to bring me closer to You, God.

Help me to receive the forgiveness that You've so freely given to me. Stop me from hurting myself and others by trying to control the disease of addiction. I am desperate to be released from its grip. I have been drowning in the consequences of my actions. I have been on death's doorstep time and again. Thank You, Father God, for helping me survive the dangers of the enemy who wants to destroy me.

Give me beauty for these ashes. Give me a burning bush moment of clarity on how to hand everything over to You. Show me what kind of good life I can have, according to Your Plan. Put me in alignment with Your Will. Guide me in Your Grace, in Your Love. Feed my spirit hope and grant every fiber of my being the knowledge that I am powerless over addiction and that my life has become unmanageable. Show me the way.

In the name of Jesus.

Amen

* * *

Dear Heavenly Father,

We come to You in desperation. We keep trying to control what we cannot control. We have been bruised and battered by the addiction. We have been face down in mud and dragged all over town, day in and day out, until we collapsed. After swearing never to pick up again, the next day we go back to the same miserable state of being in active addiction, trying to control our God-given feelings–numbing them, pushing them down or shutting them out.

God, please help our heads and our hearts see how powerless we are over addiction, that we cannot control it but rather…it controls us when we use it.

We are not God. Heavenly Father, You are God and we are not. You are All Mighty and All Powerful, and we are not.

Guide us to work the program to the best of our ability. Grant us humility, for we know little. Make us teachable and break the chains of thinking we know it all. Help us to become part of a community that understands, that welcomes us with open arms. Let our actions reflect that we cannot control anything outside of ourselves, including people, places and things. Let us take the action, on faith, to get a sponsor who will help us to navigate the program that was created to bring us closer to you, God.

Help us to receive the forgiveness that You've so freely given to us. Stop us from hurting ourselves and others through trying to control the disease of addiction. We are desperate to be released from its grip. We have been drowning in the consequences of our actions. We have been on death's doorstep time and again. Thank you, Father God, for helping us survive the dangers of the enemy who wants to destroy us.

Give us beauty for these ashes. Give us a burning bush moment of clarity on how to hand over everything to You. Show us what kind of a good life we can have, according to Your Plan. Put us in alignment with Your Will. Guide us in Your Grace, in Your Love. Feed our spirits hope and grant every fiber of our being the knowledge that we are powerless over addiction and that our lives have become unmanageable. Show us the way.

In the name of Jesus.

Amen

I was told to get a sponsor. Look for someone who has what you want.

It took me a while to gather the courage to ask someone to be my sponsor. I was so afraid of rejection that it paralyzed me. During a fellowship meeting at a coffee shop with some of the guys from the group, one gentleman suggested I take a piece of paper and list the qualities I wanted in a sponsor. I had been going to meetings for about two months and had a feel for what a sponsor was and did based on conversations during and after the meetings. That night, I put pen to paper. I put on some soft music and took a couple deep breaths, opened my eyes and started writing. I wanted someone who was kind, compassionate, could call me out on my self-deception and lies and would share their experience, strength and hope freely. Someone who was patient, loving, caring, firm. Someone with solid lengthy sobriety time. Someone with a good sense of humor, who believed in God as their Higher Power and who had integrity. I expanded my meetings and started going to two per week. It was like adding one more sober hour to my week. I was slipping and sliding pretty badly. One of these meetings was across town in Oak Park, Illinois. There was one gentleman who shared from his heart. I liked what he had to say. He was honest, open and willing to give back to the group what was freely given to him. He would do service work—lead the group conscious meetings, make coffee, organize the phone list. He conducted himself like a compassionate and successful leader, was led by the Grace of God instead of by a big ego. He told my story—the desperation, the low self-esteem, the story of a lost soul longing for connection.

He was very spiritual; in touch with God. He had a gentle yet firm tone to his voice and when he laughed, it filled the whole room and its contagious nature invited others to join in.

Finally, after a couple of months, I approached him after a meeting. I told him that I was new and that I wanted to get well. "I need to get a sponsor to do the steps. I don't want to live the life in active addiction anymore. I was wondering if you'd be my sponsor."

He smiled, looking emotionally moved, and nodded his head yes. We exchanged numbers and immediately got to work. He told me to call him every day to check in. I did and our conversations were mostly one-way streets in which I was the one talking.

From the very beginning, my recovery has been about peeling back the layers of lies to get to the truth. All active addicts are liars. It's part of the disease. Addiction is full of lies. It tells you that you're a bad person; that you don't have a problem; that you can drink like normal people; that you can use just one more time. That is why recovery demands rigorous honesty for it to have everlasting effects. In those early days of recovery, when I was relapsing all over the place, I would chat with my sponsor every day. Every time I stopped talking he would ask, "Lisa Jo, so when are you going to stop lying to yourself?"

I didn't get it for a long time. It was an unfolding process. Sometimes a series of wide and rude awakenings. An adventure from living in dishonesty to living a whole life where I didn't fool anyone anymore, including myself.

Rigorous Honesty Prayer

Dearest Heavenly Father,

Guide me out of the tunnel of lies that I tell myself—including the one that I can manage and control the addiction. Lead me out of denial. Help me become more aware of the lie that I am the one in the driver's seat when it is actually You, Jesus. I feel the gift of desperation You have given me, that my life is in shambles. Protect me as my sand castles crumble and the life that I've always known burns to the ground. Replace it with serenity and faith; deflate the cockiness and the inflated ego and replace it with humility, an open heart and a willingness to see and acknowledge that I have led a dishonest life. Break the chains of denial. Open my eyes so that I may see. Give me a shoulder to cry on when the truth hits me hard. I know, God, that crisis precedes change. Shine the light on the big shift for me as I travel from the prisons of denial into the gateways of recovery. Keep me safe. Keep me sober even when the emotions of change run high. Grant me the support of healthy recovering addicts to hold hands with as I pray for the willingness to embrace rigorous honesty. Prevent me from tricking myself into believing nothing is wrong as my life falls apart. God, You bring me to my knees as I am beginning to realize that I am powerless over my drug of choice and my life has become unmanageable. Let the truth rain down on me and show me how to live an honest life, free of compulsive behavior. Give me the gift that honesty brings, including a solid happy sobriety built upon Your Foundation of Truth.

In Jesus's name I pray,

Amen

* * *

Dearest Heavenly Father,

Guide us out of the tunnel of lies that we tell ourselves—including the one that we can manage and control the addiction. Lead us out of denial. Help us to become more aware of the lie that we are the ones in the driver's seat when it is actually You, Jesus. We are starting to feel the gift of desperation that our lives are in shambles. Protect us as our sand castles crumble and the life that we've always known burns to the ground. Replace it with serenity and faith; deflate the cockiness and the inflated ego and replace it with humility, an open heart and a willingness to see and acknowledge that we have led a dishonest life. Break the chains of denial. Open our eyes so that we may see. Give us shoulders to cry on when the truth hits us hard. We know, God, that crisis precedes change. Shine the light on the big shifts for us as we travel from the prisons of denial into the gateways of recovery. Keep us safe. Keep us sober even when the emotions of change run high. Grant us the support of healthy recovering addicts to hold hands with as we pray for the willingness to embrace rigorous honesty. Prevent us from tricking ourselves into believing nothing is wrong as our lives fall apart. God, You bring us to our knees as we are beginning to realize that we are powerless over our drug of choice and our lives have become unmanageable. Let the truth rain down on us and show us how to live an honest life, free of compulsive behavior. Give us the gifts that honesty brings, including a solid happy sobriety built upon Your foundation of Truth.

In Jesus's name we pray,

Amen

Working Step One

The first step was a raw one. It was where I faced the reality that I could not control the addiction no matter how hard I tried. I made lists of ways my life had become unmanageable, collected evidence that I was truly powerless over this disease, that it was a spiritual malady and the only way for me to have a chance of remaining clean was to realize this powerlessness on a daily basis and to develop a relationship with Christ. I had to always remind myself because this disease convinces you that you don't have a problem with addiction. The ego swoops back in and tries to control things that are not in your control.

There was a description of the phenomena of craving that a sponsor read to me from the Alcoholics Anonymous Big Book. Basically, a doctor by the name of Silkworth, believed that if you kept feeding the monster by caving into cravings, it produces more cravings. The only way off this hamster wheel and into recovery, was to first stop using.

So, that's what I did. I stopped. And immediately withdrawals rocked my world. I felt shaky and weak, life seemed bland and boring, emotions surfaced that I had been numbing for years. Suddenly, I had way too much time on my hands because the addiction had consumed all of my time before. It was like a ferocious hunger to act out. An itch I could not scratch because I was now choosing to live a sober life. I drove around aimlessly, staying off the internet because of the association with people, places and things that related to the disease of sexual compulsion.

I felt loneliness like I had never experienced before. And a deep caving in—at my heart area. At times I felt dizzy like I was coming off some crazy amusement park ride and was trying to regain my balance on solid land.

One afternoon, in the pouring rain, I was driving and the sobriety thing was too much to bear. I called my sponsor and told him that I had to act out. There was nothing I could do about it. The cravings would not get off my back, would not leave me alone. That I was going crazy.

Allen P. asked me, "What is around you?"

"There are a lot of houses and traffic and a Bed, Bath & Beyond up ahead," I said.

"Pull over into their parking lot, go inside and look at everything at Bed, Bath & Beyond."

I held on to his words for dear life and said, "Ok."

My knees were shaking as I parked and ran into the store, drenched by the rain.

The store was pretty empty on that Wednesday afternoon during the heavy rainstorm. I looked around and decided to go down every aisle in the place.

I looked at everything. The artwork, the plates, the shower curtains, the smells of different candles—ocean smells, fresh linen, lavender, peach. Looking at the walls of bric-o-brac, kitchen tools, the colorful towels that were soft to the touch. Glasses for drinking clean water or OJ in the morning. Framed pictures of sea horses and shells and cityscapes. Home decor and plaques that had positive phrases on them like "Home Sweet Home" and "Home is Where the Heart Is."

When I was done, one of God's miracles occurred. I was sober and the intense wave of excruciating cravings had passed. This was the first time I had craved so intensely and did not return to the disease to act out. I learned a valuable lesson in all this: do positive things that get you out of your head when you are stuck in it. I filled my mind with the sights and smells of candles and touch of a towel —something outside of myself that was not associated with addiction. I surrounded myself with beautiful things. The beauty impacted my perception, my mood, my level of stress.

So, instead of scratching the itch of craving, I went somewhere different in the form of a Bed, Bath & Beyond. I surrendered the craving to a suggestion my sponsor had given me. I took the chance and acted on it. It was a victory. I had became honest in admitting my powerlessness to my sponsor on that desperate day. Before I went and acted out, I called him. I picked up the heavy phone. I was honest, willing and open to trying something different. I did something different and got a different result.

I could not have done it on my own. It was me, my sponsor and God.

I have grown in my program to know that my sponsor is not God and not to be put on any pedestal. However, these relationships were vital to my recovery.

In a program that addressed compulsive overeating, I complimented my sponsor Elizabeth G. on some advice she had just given me. She was humble and answered, "It's not just me. It's a trinity: It's you, me and God." She was right. There was always guidance from above.

Like every good sponsor, she was patient with me, gentle like a feather, but firm at times. She called me out on my stuff, when I lied to myself. She said she could only share her experience, strength and hope, nothing more, nothing less. When I fell off the horse and thought she would "fire" me, she told me "We don't shoot our wounded."

Instead, she offered a hand, so I could brush myself off and keep going. I never gave up, even when I was a chronic relapser, ashamed of what I was doing to myself. And she never gave up on me. She loved me until I learned how to love myself.

She was there for me through thick and thin, through chronic relapse to gaining traction in recovery and having sobriety time. She always stressed that it is a "one day at a time program" and encouraged me not to count days since it was "just for today."

She gave me a perspective that I couldn't have seen on my own, because I was too sick. I had the disease of addiction and it lied to me in my own voice. Her advice was nearly always worth taking to see if it was effective.

She was patient, even when I rebelled against her suggestions like a wild teenager. Sponsorship is really special. It's how we best work the steps—with this loving guidance, this person who is freely giving back what was freely given to them.

Blessing a Sponsor Prayer

God,

Thank You for doing for me what I could never do alone. You gave me an opportunity to come clean of demoralizing addictive behaviors, and I took it. Thank You for giving me a safe space to do this, as my sponsor led me out of isolation and back into the stream of life. Thank You for this sacred connection.

Please bless my sponsor. Give them serenity throughout the week and laughter and relaxation. Please stay extra close to them, God. They are a great child of Yours and are helping me so much. God, guide me to be Your vehicle—work through me with gestures, kindness, empathy and love. Show me how to extend the generosity of my sponsor to others.

Give me the willingness to be teachable. Show me how to respect my sponsor, as I am learning to respect myself. I am humbly grateful that I was fortunate enough to find out what was wrong with me, before it was too late. I have so much love for You, God. Let me show this love to my fellows and to those who cross my path.

Thank You for the beautiful and powerful connection of sponsorship—this life raft, this hope. I praise You, Holy Spirit, for working through my sponsor, offering me a way out of the misery of addiction. Thy Will, not mine, be done.

In Jesus's name.

Amen

* * *

God,

Thank You for doing for us what we could never do alone. You gave us an opportunity to come clean of demoralizing addictive behaviors, and we took it. Thank You for giving us a safe space to do this, as our sponsors led us out of isolation and back into the stream of life. Thank You for this sacred connection.

Please bless our sponsors. Give them serenity throughout the week and laughter and relaxation. Please stay extra close to them, God. They are great children of Yours and are helping us so much. God, guide us to be Your vehicle—work through us with gestures, kindness, empathy and love. Show us how to extend the generosity of our sponsors to others.

Give us the willingness to be teachable. Show us how to respect our sponsors, as we are learning to respect ourselves. We are humbly grateful that we were fortunate enough to find out what was wrong with us, before it was too late. We have so much love for you, God. Let us show this love to our fellows and to those who cross our paths.

Thank you for the beautiful and powerful connection of sponsorship—this life raft, this hope. We praise You, Holy Spirit, for working through our sponsors, offering us a way out of the misery of addiction. Thy Will, not ours, be done.

In Jesus's name.

Amen

Chapter 3:

Hope in the Hills and Valleys (Step 2)

Step 2: Came to believe that a Power greater than ourselves could restore us to sanity.

My soul, wait in silence for God
For my hope is from Him.
Psalm 62:5 (NASB)

When I first came into the rooms, I didn't have a clear picture of my Higher Power. For much of my life, I called my Higher Power "The Universe." Even when I heard God talk to me in Bangkok, it didn't stop me from thinking I had to do things my way, all by myself. So, I continued to Edge God Out (EGO) of my life, the best I could. He was still there. He wasn't going anywhere. My free will was making some unhealthy choices and I began to experience the consequences of my actions. I was sick with addiction. I thought that my best thinking could get me out of this mess. What I didn't realize yet was that it was my thinking that got me into the mess to begin with.

Every time I used my drug of choice, I shut the door on God. I wanted to control and numb my feelings because I felt they were life threatening. I didn't have time to know God, or ask Him who He was. I didn't ask him what the emotions were there for. At lightening speed, I wanted to cut it short, run from discomfort, numb out and move on. I moved frantically to run away and get high. I could not catch up with myself. I was running too fast to stop and get to know who I was. I did not recognize myself when I looked in the mirror. I had become someone else.

When I sat down to do my second step work, putting pen to paper, I discovered more intimately who Almighty God was. I have heard that some people redefine what God means for them, what His qualities are for them and that this may look very different than the punishing God they grew up worshiping and being afraid of. I didn't have any preconceived notions since God was never explained to me in my family of origin. My connection was the loving, kind voice I had heard deep inside my heart when I was in Bangkok. So, coming to believe in a Higher Power required me to get to know Him better. I decided to brainstorm for this step to really have depth and impact. It was through the guidance of my sponsor that I learned who God was to me.

I sat at a café and stared at a blank piece of paper. I wrote "God" at the very top of the page, right in the center. Then I started brainstorming, not thinking too much so that what was in my heart could come out.

God as I understand Him, is a loving caring God who always wants the best for me. He protects me with all of His Might. I am His child. He is my Creator; He is always there for me and has infinite compassion for me in my journey.

How does God communicate with me? He usually speaks to me in a quiet, steady and clear voice. The Holy Spirit works through my intuition. I can often hear His Words, sometimes through the sound of my own voice, deep inside of my heart but calm. Sometimes it's a feeling in my gut. When I get quiet, His Words come to me and the volume is higher and slightly louder.

The Holy Spirit comes to me as a thought or inspiration and is also transmitted through other people. He has created intricate lines of communication. Sometimes when I am in the rooms of the program, I hear the message directly through another person's share. In addition, He expresses His Knowledge, Wisdom and Guidance through symbols and other living things.

Jesus is the Prince of Peace, the Author, the Beginner and the Finisher, my Deliverer, the Light of the World, my Redeemer, the Lamb of God. Jesus is tranquil and calm like a still clear lake. All love. He is solidly peaceful and friendly, strong and serene. His Hedge of Protection is always comforting. I can always rely on God. He is both graceful and has a great sense of humor. He takes away loneliness and fear. He guides me into the present moment. He astounds me by showering me with prosperity, abundance, love, wealth, money, joy, a good life. He performs miracle after miracle.

God fulfills my prayers in His Own Time. God's timing is perfect, even when I cannot see the bigger picture at the moment. It is always for my good.

God enjoys when I talk to Him. The more specific I can be, the better. Prayer becomes a promise to God, for me to do God's Will. God's Inspiration fills my mind and actions with positive intention. He pushes me to act on the prayers that I have spoken. Sometimes to meet Him halfway.

God is my partner, my cheerleader, my Great Counselor. He is my greatest support. His guidance and inspiration are All Powerful.

God is Great. Greater than anything I could ever have imagined. I am in awe.

After writing this, I longed for a closer relationship with Him. I put down on paper how He had literally restored me to sanity. It was literal sanity. He brought me back from the madness of a bipolar psychotic manic episode.

I was born with the disease of Bipolar I and Complex PTSD, which is a severe anxiety disorder. I have experienced severe suicidal depressions several times in my life. Anxiety and depression seem to go hand in hand.

My anxiety levels frequently skyrocketed. My addictions have been partially about self-medicating the symptoms of mental disease, because my emotional life was very unstable in my teens, 20s and 30s. I was just holding on, just surviving. In a strange way, the drug use and sex addiction saved my life. Without obliterating my emotions, as they did, I probably would have killed myself.

While living in Chicago, during the worst depression I had ever experienced, I started mixing hardcore drugs with the sex addiction. I needed to drown out everything in order to survive.

God literally restored me to sanity. Today, God shows me, through a lot of trial and error, how to be a stable and responsible member of society. I don't blame my problems on my mental health, something I used to do to a fault. God granted me house ownership, prosperity and wealth in all forms, love beyond reason and emotional stability that I never thought was possible, a rewarding day job that was hard rewarding work with good pay.

When I was 21 years old, I had my first psychotic manic episode in San Francisco. I lost control of my mind. I stayed awake for weeks and my ego became so inflated, I thought I was all-powerful. I was delusional. I had grandiose behavior that was over the top.

Even though I went to San Francisco to visit with a friend from high school, I spent most of my time on the streets day and night in the Haight-Ashbury neighborhood, which was famous in the 60s for hippies hanging out doing drugs, having anti-war protests during the "summer of love."

One night a man followed me at 3 o'clock in the morning. I could hear his footsteps, it was like a horror movie. I would cross an empty street and his footsteps followed me. I started running until I found another stranger sitting on the corner, who looked at the guy following me, and told him to leave me alone. God was watching out for me.

I had hallucinations both audio and visual, even when I wasn't high. I was totally delusional. I was not aware of what was happening, because this had never happened before. I sold my bus ticket back to Arizona, where I lived at the time, and took a public bus back to Haight-Ashbury. I got off the bus and there was a man folding clothes and putting them into a grocery shopping cart. Without asking, I started helping him fold and pile the clothes to the rim. It was a stray Safeway cart. I put my backpack on top of all the clothes. He told me–hop in. I did.

He pushed me down a big hill to Golden Gate Park. I never knew his name–he was just a "friendly" stranger along my journey of insanity. He kissed me and we had sex ten feet from traffic in broad daylight. Afterward, I got paranoid and pushed the grocery cart with all of his clothes and all my belongings, into the middle of the street, and yelled, "Leave me alone!"

He did. I never saw him or my belongings again.

I took a taxi back to Berkeley where a toxic lover lived. I did not have any money for the cab fare. The taxi driver called the cops. I was arrested and on the way to the police station, I began talking about the thought police. The cops changed directions and headed straight to the nearest psych ward. Thank God for those policemen who helped save my life. I could not distinguish who was a safe person and who was dangerous. My intuition wasn't working right. It is very dangerous to have untreated bipolar, especially when having a manic or depressive episode. They were life-threatening. Those cops were really angels sweeping me off the dangerous streets of San Francisco before something horribly tragic happened.

I wasn't diagnosed with Bipolar I until I was back in Denver. My parents loved me so much that they flew out to get me from the hospital in Berkeley. I was really upset with them at the time. I thought they were trying to control me. They were really saving my life.

Looking forward, it was only by the grace of God that I have learned how to manage these conditions through staying close to Him, getting to know myself, learning new coping skills and taking a cocktail of medication daily. Because God restored me to sanity in one area meant that he can restore me to sanity in all areas of my life, including giving me freedom from the insanity of addiction.

I began to have faith. By working the second step, I discovered a lot about God's good nature. He had it not just some of the time, but always. Through exploring my faith in recovery, I started believing the reality that my sins had already been forgiven. That I didn't have to reside in the darkness of shame. This began my journey of self-forgiveness. Step 2 was the beginning of hope.

⚜

God's Hope Prayer

God,

Reveal the vastness of Your Glory. Show me ways to get to know You. Let me carry Your Vision into all that I do. Speak directly into my heart. Let Your Wonderful Magnificence flow through the ink in my pen onto the paper of my second step work. Show me Your equanimity, Your Abiding Love. Let me always recognize Your Divine Grace in every moment. Transform my life. Give me wings like eagles and the courage to take flight out of the ugly pits of addiction. Help me understand the different ways that only You can restore me to sanity. The Word tells me that I can do anything through Christ. I want to know that freedom, God.

I praise You for single-handedly leading me into the program. Inspire me to help others, to begin to know that I can only keep what I give away. Thank you, God, for saving my life. Hold me strong in Your Grace: open my eyes to the great plan You have for me. Impact all of my decisions.

Dear Lord, I want to see You clearly. Show me the truthful ways that I am Your masterpiece. Show me how to put everything into Your Hands. You are on the throne. Not any person, place or thing. Jesus, I make you my Lord and Savior. I receive beauty for these ashes. I open my eyes to see you clearly working in my life. I have come to believe in your All-Encompassing Power. You flung stars into space and created worlds. You gave me my first breath and You will give me my last. Keep my hands open so that You can flow through me, Holy Spirit. Lift me out of the ruins of self-destruction into a redeemed and beautiful restoration of my sanity.

In Jesus's Name,

Amen

* * *

God,

Reveal the vastness of Your Glory. Show us how to get to know You. Let us carry Your Vision into all that we do. Speak directly into our hearts. Let Your Wonderful Magnificence flow through the ink in our pens onto the paper of our second step work. Show us Your Equanimity, Your abiding love. Let us always recognize Your Divine Grace in every moment.

Transform our lives. Give us wings like eagles and the courage to take flight out of the ugly pits of addiction. Help us understand the different ways that only You can restore us to sanity. The Word tells us that we can do anything through Christ. We want to know that freedom, God.

We praise You for single-handedly leading us into the program. Inspire us to help others, to begin to know that we can only keep what we give away. Thank You, God, for saving our lives. Hold us strong in Your Grace: open our eyes to the great plans You have for us. Impact our every decision. Dear Lord, we want to see You clearly. Show us the truth that we are Your masterpiece. Show us how to put everything into Your Hands. You are on the throne. Not any person, place or thing. Jesus, we make You our Lord and Savior. We receive beauty for the ashes of misery. We open our hands to see You clearly working in our lives. We have come to believe in Your All-Encompassing Power. You flung stars into space and created worlds. You gave us our first breath and You will give us our last. Keep our hands open so that You can flow through us. Lift us out of the ruins of self-destruction into a redeemed and beautiful restoration of our sanity.

In Jesus's Name,

Amen

A Step of Hope

The guiding principle of Step 2 is HOPE. Step 1 revealed there was a real distorted belief that I had to do everything on my own. There was a stubborn spirit of being independent and that I needed to prove to myself that I could do it all my way. I tried to do it this way for years and it just didn't work. Human beings are not islands. We need connection and guidance from a Higher Power. "That one is God, may you find Him now" as the Alcoholics Anonymous book reads in the chapter *How it Works*.

The solution to recovering from the devastation of active addiction had to involve a power greater than ourselves. Getting out of the cycle of self-destruction and shame was too much for one person to handle, but with the help of Almighty God, we had a chance at living a wonderful life, filled with hope and faith and connection.

This reminds me of the "ABC's" in the chapter ***How It Works*** in the AA Big Book, that makes clear three pertinent ideas:

A. "That we were alcoholic and could not manage our own lives."
B. "That probably no human power could have relieved our alcoholism."
C. "That God could and would if He were sought."

Hope lets God in and knowing that by self-will alone, we will always stumble and fall. But with God, anything is possible, including recovery from addiction. Hope also comes from connecting to others and hearing their stories, made possible by joining a meeting.

There were too many times to count on my hands that I resisted going to a meeting, by avoiding it or simply, making the decision to go out and use instead. When I did make it to a meeting, I always felt 100% better. Something about connecting to others and being in that safe space with friendly faces, all telling versions of the story I lived. I was not alone. It healed me. If I went to a meeting for an hour, that was one hour I was not using my drug of choice. The more meetings I went to, the more I wanted to be plugged into the solution. I could talk to people before and after the meetings, have fellowship with others outside the meetings, exchange numbers and call people I met in meetings, to get help when I needed it. In the rooms, we were never alone, and I am not only thankful for in-person meetings, but truly grateful to God for the virtual meetings as well, making it possible to go to a meeting no matter what time of day it was from the comfort of my home. Recovery around the clock, by God's Mighty Grace.

Going to a Meeting Prayer

Dear God,

Help me to take action to get to a meeting on time. Guide me to pay attention, focus, and to actively listen. Open my eyes to honesty, openness and a willingness when I share. Help me to make new program friends, to talk to people before and after the meeting with an open heart. Show me how to be a sponge absorbing Your Wisdom through the voices of others.

Shine Your Light like a bright star, so I can recognize The Holy Spirit in the eyes of other recovering addicts, as they sit down in the chairs around me and speak. Teach me through other's shares the depth and understanding of surrender, faith and honesty. Grant me attention to the richness found in the experience, strength and hope, confessions, the tears of apprehension and worry, the laughter of glory and celebration, all shared by my recovery brothers and sisters sitting around me. Tune me into You, Holy Spirit, as we all work together to actively be in conscious contact with You through working the 12-step program and by staying connected to each other.

In Jesus's name I pray.

Amen

* * *

Dear God,

Help us to take action to get to a meeting on time. Guide us to pay attention, focus, and to actively listen. Open our eyes to honesty, openness and a willingness when we share. Help us to make new program friends, to talk to people before and after the meeting with an open heart. Show us how to be a sponge absorbing Your Wisdom through the voices of others.

Shine Your Light like a bright star, so we can recognize The Holy Spirit in the eyes of other recovering addicts, as they sit down in the chairs around us and speak. Teach us through other's shares the depth and understanding of surrender, faith and honesty. Grant us attention to the richness found in the experience, strength and hope, confessions, the tears of apprehension and worry, the laughter of glory and celebration, all shared by our recovery brothers and sisters sitting around us. Tune us into You, Holy Spirit, as we all work together to actively be in conscious contact with You through working the 12-step program and by staying connected to each other.

In Jesus's name we pray.

Amen

Now that I gained clarity on what my Higher Power, God, meant to me, I was ready to take the third step, making the decision to surrender my life and my will to Him.

Chapter 4:

Surrendering to God (Step 3)

Step 3: Made a decision to turn our will and our lives over the care of God *as we understood Him*.

Therefore humble yourselves under
The mighty hand of God, that He may
Exalt you at the proper time.
1 Peter 5:6 (NASB)

All action begins with a decision. We cannot skip this and move directly into action. In order to surrender our lives and our wills over to God, we must first make a decision to do so. This decision is a total gamechanger. A lifesaver. I stopped attempting to solve things on my own. Instead, I opened the door and consciously let God in.

"Made a decision" is a turning point. It is a lifestyle change that you are consciously deciding to bring God into your life in an active way. It means making the courageous decision to let God direct you. Praying regularly will allow Him in to show you the way. Once the decision is made, it is just a matter of time before your actions align with God's best for you.

It is the foundation from which transformation can begin, to feel freedom from addiction, on a daily basis, because we know in our hearts that using the drug of our choice is not God's Will for us. He does not want us to destroy ourselves and negatively impact those around us.

At first, I was terrified at the thought of handing things over. I always operated out of self-will. I stubbornly tried to exert my control over everything in order to feel in control. I mourned the loss of that sense of control, even though it was an illusion. My self-will felt like the glue that held me together. I was never going to have to "go it alone" again, but my ego cried out like an anthem, "But I can do this alone. I must prove to the world and to myself that I can handle it; that I can fix, manipulate and rescue myself in isolation. I must save myself by using my own will only. I don't need God's help!"

The addiction is a liar. Deciding to take the leap of faith to let God fully work in my life, was one of the most important decisions I ever made. Even as it is vital to our recovery, it is not a one-and-done deal. As a recovering addict, I resorted to taking back my will back from God plenty of times, and still do. It's part of being human. It's a program of progress not perfection.

Acting on self-will alone is the "easy road" that actually has the hardest consequences. "Easy," meaning predictable, comes naturally; easy to do, is your go-to. Letting go and letting God is the "hardest road" yet the path that is full of miracles. It is hard to align with God's Will through the act of surrender, especially at first, because it means change, and change is hard. It has to be a decision you make with your heart as well as your head. We addicts don't like to feel things, and often end up intellectualizing things to death, getting stuck in our own heads.

My decision to hand my will over, combined with letting God transform my faith into action was powerful; it was an entire paradigm shift. It meant living and flowing with life on life's terms.

Of course, as a human being, I don't always understand why things happen. As an active addict, I wanted to control everything and to know exactly and precisely how things were going to pan out. I tried to "run the show," ignoring that God is the driver's seat, not me. I am merely the passenger.

In early recovery, when there was a crisis or if something was not going MY way, I became overwhelmed—crawling out of my skin and triggered to want to use. If I were to go back out, I could have the illusion of control with my drug of choice, when in reality, I was powerless over it. Completely powerless.

Recovery teaches us how to flow with life, instead of painful attempts to swim upstream against the current, trying desperately to control outcomes. Surrendering to living life on life's terms is a gateway to peace.

God's plans are much bigger than mine. He closes one door in order to open another. There is a trust that develops over time. God is running the show and I can rest in that faith. Living life on life's terms has a solid and serene flow to it, though it is not always comfortable. Fear miraculously disappears when you put your total faith in God. Acceptance is the key to all my problems.

Life on Life's Terms Prayer

Dear Father God,

Grow my faith in You. Come into the fire with me. I may not like what is happening; what is going on in my life. I may be in emotional pain. Help me to see that I am never alone, that You are always with me, no matter how much happiness, sorrow, grief or satisfaction I am feeling. Let me trust that You are unfolding life according to Your Plan. Help me to flow with Your Plan even when I don't understand it. I surrender my will and my life to You, dear Lord. I ask to comprehend the opportunities You give me, to rest in Your Hands, and feel the serenity You offer me as I flow with life on life's terms. I have faith that Your Way, God, is the best way and is part of Your Bigger Plan, that everything happens for a reason. Let me learn my lessons well. Thank you for the sacred lessons You have taught me. Let me get out of my head by being present for others, even when I don't like what is going on in my own life. Give me strength. Grow my faith in Your Plans for me, knowing there is a higher reason. Come into the fire with me. Show me how to navigate through situations I don't like. Give me conscious awareness, an eye for all the beauty that You place in my path. There is purpose in all things. There are no accidents in Your World, God. Let me always submit and have faith for living life on life's terms, the way You have planned for me. Thank You for giving me this life to live, to learn the lessons You teach to make me a better person.

In the name of Jesus,

Amen

* * *

Dear Father God,

Grow our faith in You. Come into the fire with us. We may not like what is happening; what is going on in our lives. We may be in emotional pain. Help us to see that we are never alone, that You are always with us, no matter how much happiness, sorrow, grief or satisfaction we are feeling. Let us trust that You are unfolding life according to Your Plan. Help us to flow with Your Plan even when we don't understand it. We surrender our will and our lives to You, dear Lord. We ask to comprehend the opportunities You give us, to rest in Your Hands, and feel the serenity You offer us as we flow with life on life's terms. We have faith that Your Way, God, is the best way and is part of Your Bigger Plan, that everything happens for a reason. Let us learn our lessons well. Thank you for the sacred lessons You have taught us. Let us get out of our heads by being present for others, even when we don't like what is going on in our own lives. Give us strength. Grow our faith in Your Plans for us, knowing there is a higher reason. Show us how to navigate through situations we don't like. Give us conscious awareness, an eye for all the beauty that You place in our path. There is purpose in all things. There are no accidents in Your World, God. Let us always submit and have faith for living life on life's terms, the way You have planned for us. Thank You for giving us these lives to live, to learn the lessons You teach to make us better people.

In the name of Jesus,

Amen

Prior to working the program, I wanted to do things my way or the highway. I aimed to prove that I could do everything by myself and that I could handle putting myself in both triggering and dangerous situations, and manage to stay afloat. This self-reliance got my wheels spinning nowhere fast. This stubborn self-reliance was not the answer.

The third step was a mustard seed and a gigantic leap of faith all at once. It took a little bit of faith to make a decision to turn my life and will over to the care of God, as I understood him. It was a leap of faith to actually commit to action, really opening up to the possibility of handing over my will and life to Almighty God, and to begin to surrender. It made me very nervous for a while. It meant a decision and then later action to surrendering EVERYTHING. My decisions, my heartaches, my ways, my sorrows, my strategies and my world views. All of it. There is a phrase that says "God is God and I'm not." Only God can heal me. I can't do it on self-will alone. I need His help. Without Him, it is not possible. No human power could relieve me of out of control insanity. Only God could. I wake up and praise God every day for giving me another day in recovery.

Taking the Third Step

When I took my third step, I was at an AA club. I was on the second floor, down on one knee, holding my sponsor's hand. With my eyes closed, I began reciting the third step prayer out loud, I adore this prayer. It is so rich with spiritual meaning. My favorite line in this prayer is:

> God:
> " ...Take away my difficulties
> That victory over them may bear witness
> To those I would help of **Thy Power, Thy Love and Thy Way of Life**."

As I recited the prayer by heart, it felt like the weight I had carried my whole life was lifted. Now, I could look God in the eye and ask for the help I needed. By taking the third step, I felt a surrender from trying to manage things on my own to putting it all in God's hands. I could now take action on this decision by letting go and letting God. I could stay sober by God's grace every hour and every second of every day, one hour and one day at a time. It all started with faith and the decision contained in the third step.

Raise the White Flag Prayer

God,

After this long and winding rocky road, bring ease to my recovery. Show me the willingness to be willing to hand over all my compulsive thoughts, actions and fears. Dear Lord, remind me that I cannot control the addiction; that I am truly powerless over it. Give me strength to trust in You; to raise the white flag as high as an eagle can fly, fully giving my life and my will to You.

Bless me with the clarity of taking the next best indicated step. Show me how to listen to Your soft, yet steady voice; to be receptive to Your Intuitive Thought or Inspiration. Help me to break through all forms of resistance. Help me to obey Your Loving Direction. Be there for me as I become more vibrant in my awareness so I can feel

You as You hold my hands during difficult times. Show me that I will never be alone again. For You are always with me.

Dear Lord, I praise you for the miracles of recovery, of leading me out of the dark depths of hell, for giving me back focus, joy and satisfaction. Thank You for filling my heart with love and gratitude. Grant me clear opportunities to reach out and provide a helping hand to those in need. Bring me fun and laughter throughout my days. Grow my connection to others. Place true friends in my path. Transform the struggle into an empowering enjoyable journey of healing.

Always guide me back to You when I start taking my will back. Guide me through life on life's terms and grow my faith in You and Your Plans. Help me be patient. I am Your passenger. You are the Driver. You are my CEO, my Great Employer; I pray for the willingness to be willing to surrender control to You, God. Flow through my words, my emotional expressions, my actions. Let me be of service to others and let Your Love shine through every interaction I have. Show me how You have a great purpose for me. Take me to new heights in my recovery that I cannot even imagine today.

In Jesus's Name.

Amen

* * *

God,

After this long winding rocky road, bring ease to our recovery. Show us the willingness to be willing to hand over all our compulsive thoughts, actions and fears. Dear Lord, remind us that we cannot control the addiction; that we are truly powerless over it. Give us strength to trust in You; to raise the white flag as high as an eagle can fly, fully giving our lives and our wills to You.

Bless us with the clarity of taking the next best indicated step. Show us how to listen to Your soft, yet steady voice; to be receptive to Your Intuitive Thought or Inspiration. Help us to break through all forms of resistance. Help us to obey Your Loving Direction. Be there for us as we become more vibrant in our awareness so we can feel You as You hold our hands during difficult times. Show us that we will never be alone again. For You are always with us.

Dear Lord, I praise You for the miracles of recovery, of leading us out of the dark depths of hell, for giving us back focus, joy and satisfaction. Thank You for filling our hearts with love and gratitude. Grant us clear opportunities to reach out and provide a helping hand to those in need. Bring us fun and laughter throughout my days. Grow our connections to others. Place true friends in our paths. Transform the struggle into an empowering enjoyable journey of healing.

Always guide us back to you when we start taking our wills back. Guide us through life on life's terms and grow our faith in You and Your Plans. Help us be patient. We are Your passengers. You are the Driver. You are our CEO, our Great Employer; We pray for the willingness to be willing to surrender control to You, God. Flow through our words, our emotional expressions, our actions. Let us be of service to others and let Your Love shine through every interaction we have. Show us how You have a great purpose for us. Take us to new heights in our recovery that we cannot even imagine today.

In Jesus's Name.

Amen

Years after I had taken my third step, as a sponsor, I guided a sponsee through her own third step. At one of our weekly meetings, she read me what her Higher Power's wonderful qualities were, after meditating on it and doing some mindful writing.

We went to a park in the middle of the city on a hot summer afternoon. We scouted out a park bench with flowers nearby, overlooking a lake. We breathed together in the silence, just being present. It was a trinity—her, me and God. I felt God nearby, cradling us in His Loving Presence. I spoke a prayer I had written to inspire her on her recovery journey. She then knelt in the grass on one knee, held my hand and recited the third step prayer. I bore witness as this woman accepted God into her heart as the Great Guidance in her life. How transformative and emotional the experience was for the both of us. It changed her life, just as it had changed mine. It was amazing doing service work sponsoring other people. It was like going through the steps again and again. It's a wonderful process. I renewed my own commitment to living in the third step, surrendering my will and handing over my life to Him.

Chapter 5:

How Not to Work
the Fourth Step

Now faith is the assurance of
Things hoped for, the conviction
Of things not seen.
Hebrews 11:1 (NASB)

Resentments are like taking poison and expecting the other person to die. The AA Big Book says, "Resentment is the number one offender. It destroys more alcoholics than anything else."

Most of us have a ton of resentments coming into Step 4. I didn't quite know what to do with all of them, even though I had been given sheets to fill out–to list all my resentments in one neat column, then listing what happened (or answering the question, What made me mad?) in a second column.

The columns looked nice and neat. My brain and emotional state was not. I felt the bitterness of my resentments and it looked messy. Starting an inventory brought more and more of the discomfort and anger of my resentments to the surface. It was an overwhelming and intense time. Living in Chicago. I experienced the most severe and suicidal depression I ever had. I was frequently going in and out of hospitals, in-patient and in the group therapy of Intensive Outpatient Programs. I was barely staying afloat by going to meetings, doing fellowship and seeing my sponsor.

I just scratched the surface of my held resentments when I started taking my will back. My prayer life suffered. I forgot that I had made a decision to turn my life and my will over to the care of God. I even started forgetting about God, and his Everlasting Love.

I hadn't realized that in order to bravely move through a fourth step without acting out, you need to lean into Step 3—into placing all resentments, all feelings, all memories, into the hands of God. To surrender it all.

I began to wander in and out of the rooms, with one foot in and one foot out of the program. I started isolating and making excuses not to go to meetings. I started trying to control things. My strong program slipped. It seemed so gradual at first.

It felt like I had lost the ability to be thorough; that I could not take the program seriously, as if my life depended on it. I started hanging around people, places and things associated with using my drugs of choice, not thinking I would fall into the rabbit hole. Seeing if I "could handle it." I was not relying upon God, which is what I needed to do to make it through in one piece.

I was not willing to completely release the grip that I had on doing things my way. I stopped following the direction and guidance of my sponsor and my fellows.

After my first major relapse, I learned that everything must be uncovered, uprooted and examined through a lens of honesty. No half-truths, no weak efforts. I had to put my body and my soul into this program if I was ever going to recover, one day at a time. It was about progress, not perfection, but honesty did not seem to be optional. I had to get myself planted in a church community and 12-step meetings. I had to emotionally stop entertaining and glamorizing my drugs of choice. I needed to get on the spirituality train and start trusting Christ more than I trusted myself.

As addicts, we are liars. We don't want to do anything hard except get a substance to escape reality with, to obliterate what is real. We are very sick people. Honest-to-God, hard work seemed impossible with this disease. How was I to muster up the strength and energy to work the steps and do a thorough inventory, not skipping or sweeping anything under the rug, when I was busy getting high?

I had to ask for help from other people and from my Lord Jesus Christ. It was only by taking it one day at a time that I had the ability to do that. I could do some step work–just for today. I could go to a meeting–just for today. I could look at myself more honestly, just for today. I could surrender all the cravings and the euphoric recall to God–just for today. Just for today, I can obey God's guidance and know that His Way is for my greatest good–to grow and to have Him transform my misery into freedom, bring me beauty for my ashes. But first, I had to let go of the ashes. I had to let go and let God. I had to grow my faith.

Half Measures Availed Us Nothing Prayer

Father God,

Place both my feet into recovery. Give me the courage to step in with both feet, instead of keeping one foot in and one foot out. Help me to make a commitment. Grant me the strength and energy to work a strong program and not rest on my laurels. Bring my eyes to areas where I am slacking and help me to get into alignment with Your Will. Take me into a rewarding, happy life of integrity. Show me that I must clean up my side of the street in order to obtain serenity. Keep me from numbing out, from avoidance, from living full-time in the past or the future. Let me identify my emotions and feel them in my body without going back to the drug. Give me strength to cry out, to laugh, to identify and feel in the present. Let my experiences wash over me and let me be there for them fully, trusting God, with both feet in.

In Christ's name I pray.

Amen

* * *

Father God,

Place both our feet into recovery. Give us the courage to step in with both feet, instead of keeping one foot in and one foot out. Help us make a commitment. Grant us the strength and energy to work a strong program and not rest on our laurels. Bring our eyes to areas where we are slacking and help us to get into alignment with Your Will. Take us into a rewarding, happy life of integrity. Show us that we must clean up our side of the street in order to obtain serenity. Keep us from numbing out, from avoidance, from living full-time in the past or the future. Let us identify our emotions and feel them in our bodies without going back to the drug. Give us strength to cry out, to laugh, to identify and feel the present. Let our experiences wash over us and let us be there for them fully, trusting God, with both feet in.

In Christ's name I pray.

Amen

I was drained and over-drugged under the guidance of an incompetent psychiatrist for unmanageable severe bipolar depression. I went down the rabbit hole and started using again. The addiction picked up right where it left off and got worse.

There began a more aggressive search for sex with strangers, now in public places—during the day and night. I experienced a heightened thrill of possibly getting caught. I was breaking the law.

In the past, I made sure to always meet men in public first, but this time I broke all my rules. It started when I posted an ad and ended up walking into a stranger's dark house. I had sex with him and left without ever seeing what he looked like.

This led me to the darkest ego-driven period of my life. I was desperate to self-medicate my mental health conditions since they were getting worse. With an inflated ego, I shut God out and went places I never imagined going.

The Dark Adventures of a Snow Bunny

The first time I did cocaine was behind a strip mall in Denver's Capitol Hill. I wasn't impressed by the effect. I felt nothing.

I was at the ripe old age of 16 when I was smoking pot regularly and dropping acid every Friday night at an all-age Gothic and Punk nightclub. Cocaine as a teen didn't offer me any kind of high.

For my best friend, Jennifer, it was another story. She loved being all coked up, her shy personality vanished, giving way to a talkative giddy socialite.

We would wander in and out of different men's homes together, where I'd watch her waiting patiently while the guy broke up white powder with a credit card, making it the smooth consistency of sparkling snow.

Now, after working a weak 12-step program, were I stopped going to meetings altogether, hard drugs began to appeal to me. I needed something stronger than what I was doing to get high. I was considering falling off into a new oblivion and putting myself at risk for drug addiction. Depressed, in a spiraling pit, I desperately needed to get away from the excruciating emotional pain in my head.

I remembered an old party-line, an old-school "find a friend" telephone line, which was "always free for women."

I dialed the number. How it works is you record a voicemail-like profile introducing yourself and what you are looking for. Then you get to listen to the profiles of men who were also on the line. If you liked a certain one, you could send them a private voice message back. I quickly juggled a bunch of men at once, in an insane attempt to chase a higher high and to get sex quicker so that I could jump up, get out of my bed which I had been in for days on end, take a shower, get all dolled up with layers of beautiful striking make-up, dresses and high heels and wait for them to arrive.

Sex was the only thing that inspired me to get out of bed. There, I could leave the old depressed me behind and put on a false persona. I relied on it—the persona of a sexy, confident, sassy, ravishingly beautiful, powerful woman. Impeccable. Solid. I didn't feel that way on the inside, but I sure did look good. I smoked a cigarette, waited for the men to come to me.

The big downfall of the party phone line is that you don't get to see what the people look like before meeting them. Usually, the men on those lines were full of short pickings. But a persistent hardcore addict like me was known to score and score hard.

As I was listening to the voicemail posts from the men, one man caught my attention asking if any of the women knew how to "ski." We started messaging back and forth. He asked me if I wanted to "hit the slopes." I had seen this lingo before on internet hook-up sites. For years I had dismissed these ads because I thought I was too old to start a drug habit, and I still cared about my body, my mind and my soul to a certain extent.

Now I just wanted to chase a higher high. I fastened my seatbelt to give cocaine another try. Nothing else mattered. It didn't matter that I was nearly 40, or that my sex addiction was already trying to kill me. I knew instinctively that I was playing with fire, and there was a good chance I was going to get burned. These lies rationalized that there was a thrilling, heavenly escape in my future. My excitement and anticipation was off the chart. Sex and hard drugs. Like a cliche. I had been a musician at an earlier place in my life. "Sex, drugs and rock n' roll." I thought to myself in the quiet dead of night, "Let's see how good these two things get along. Let's see what happens if I mix sex with cocaine."

I immediately went to it, interacting with the man wanting to hit the slopes. I was a natural snow bunny adept in drug lingo–a new language I had to learn to get what I wanted. I discovered with the man on the line, the first drug ad I responded to, and followed through on. It was the score of all scores. He said two magical words: "eight ball."

I didn't know exactly what that entailed, but I envisioned an exorbitant mountain of white snow.

What I didn't know at the time was that this was enough stuff to "party" all night with; definitely enough for two people,

When people say that "all addicts want to do is party," they don't get it. There is no fun in "partying" at this caliber. It was not anything like a party for me. All I wanted was to numb the pain. I didn't care what the consequences were.

His name was Chris. He left me a private message. He said that I'm perfect and he'd love to come over and hang out with me and that he had plenty of supplies and would love it if I'd be his snow bunny tonight. We hit it off. I gave him my phone number, confirming he had supplies and good looks. He said he'd be over in an hour.

As soon as I got off the phone, I jumped in the shower. I got extra clean and dressed up. My makeup was impeccable. My depression was melting off me with every passing moment. My breath was shallow with the excitement of a new adventure. My last move was the jewelry. I was all ready and I still had 30 minutes to go. I was crawling out of my skin with loneliness and anticipation. I sat on my cream-colored leather couch in my clean apartment and waited. I walked to the kitchen and sat all my teas on the counter. I thought it would be a nice gesture to make him a cup of tea. After all, he was bringing over a big mountain of expensive hard drugs.

Chris called me upon arrival because my doorbell was broken. This was the first time that I was meeting him—in the comfort of my own home. I didn't bother meeting him in public first. I thought that would just waste precious time. I needed to get to the drugs faster.

I had one main concern. What if he was ugly? That just wouldn't do.

I walked down a flight of creaky stairs. When I caught a glimpse of him, I was pleasantly surprised. He was actually very good looking: a musician with dirty blond hair and a super cool, spiritual vibe. When we got into my apartment, he looked me in the eyes and kissed me and said that he liked my energy. He not only brought sensual kisses, but charm, an entertaining personality, big fat high quality joints and an eight ball of cocaine.

He gave me instructions, and we worked together as a team. He knew I was not well versed in cocaine. This was the first time since my lame high school experience.

I did what he said. I got out a dinner plate. He piled a mountain of powder onto it, then started crushing it up with a credit card. He laid out six lines on one side of the plate. He rolled up a twenty dollar bill and handed it to me. That was my green light to go. I hesitated for a moment. Then I let go of all my concerns and fears and was ready to get high as a kite with this cute man. I snorted three lines. Chris was now my best friend. We were soul mates. I asked if I could do the other lines. "Yes," he said.

I did the other three and the feelings of intimacy and intensity increased.

My heart was beating faster. I tasted bitterness in the back of my throat and I had constant sniffles from that point forward all through the night. He stayed with me until around 6:00 a.m. We'd get all coked up and then we'd share a joint to take the edge off. We'd kiss and he'd hold me for what seemed like an eternity. Then he'd get up and lay out more lines. Bring them over to me, pass me the rolled up twenty and I'd blast off again. We listened to Zero7's *Simple Things* all night. We did all sorts of crazy things that night. Things I would have never thought of unless I was this high. We hung out all night on my twin bed.

One of the best parts of the night were the kisses that marked one activity to another. Whether it was something sexual or drugs to drugs or sex to sex or drugs to sex. There were always really fantastic erotic kisses between us. I thought we made a cute couple. Maybe we'd get married and travel someday. Then I thought to myself that I really didn't know him. He could be anyone, and so could I. I deliberately and successfully sealed up many facts about myself, hid them away like deep dark secrets that he'd never find out about.

My main attraction to strangers, and having anonymous sex, was that I could puff up feathers of an inflated ego on the outside, sporting a fake confidence that was believable, or so I thought. It made me forget how dreadfully depressed and suicidal I truly was. It was all about attempting to control how people saw me, numbing out all my God-given feelings and emotions. I was so far away from God. I forgot how to live life on God's terms. I was just fearful and desperate to manufacture a semblance of control and power. A mirage. An illusion. I was drowning in "self-will run riot." But then there was God, looking over me, patiently waiting for me to let him in again. .

Chris put on his coat and left, sealing our departure with a kiss. I didn't want him to go. But the cocaine was gone and he was going on to bigger and better things. We had conquered the holy mountain together, splitting an entire eight ball of cocaine. I was hooked.

The minute he left, I felt unbearably and painfully lonely.

I got back on the phone line, broadcasting my innocence and how I'd love to be someone's snow bunny for a while. It was my lucky day. A massage therapist named John said he had an eight ball of coke and wanted to come over right away, bright and early. I said, "Sure."

He arrived and was not nearly as cute as the other guy. He had facial hair. Yuck. But he had an eight ball of cocaine. Fun.

I was "tweaking" from doing so much of the drug that night. I was paranoid and anxious. The sounds above me didn't sound familiar and I thought that it was a police raid. John comforted me by holding me and telling me that people were just getting ready for work. That it was quarter 'til 7:00 a.m. That my neighbors didn't suspect a thing about my house, or what was going on inside. I had thought that the cops were going to kick down my door and arrest me for being high.

I asked him where the cocaine was. He got it out and asked for a plate. I reached for the same one as before. I wiped my finger across it and put it in my mouth. I could taste the bitter metallic taste of the coke from mountain number one.

I was not only addicted to sex now, but also to snow.

I sensed immediately that John thought I was more attractive than I thought he was. Usually this was a big turn-off. But there was an eight ball involved, another high mountain of cocaine to snort. So I pretended, manipulated, seduced. I pushed forward with it. I watched him prepare. I watched with every cell in my body, the ritual before the use. I waited eagerly for him to hand me the rolled up twenty dollar bill. And then he did.

That was the green light.

We started doing lines like they were going out of style. I put on some music. Zero7's album *Simple Things*. It became the soundtrack of my drug addiction.

John was a really friendly guy. I began to relax. He said he wanted to give me a full-body massage and said that he was a certified massage therapist. I couldn't say no. But I suggested that we get high first. It was cocaine serendipity. He formed eight lines and handed me the twenty. In less than two minutes, I had done them all. I was climbing another mountain.

Chris, cocaine guy number one, had left me some "party favors"—four big joints of really good pot. I suggested we light one up. I was feeling quite paranoid and didn't know if this would calm me down or make it worse. It helped a little. I was in another world. One of sexual freedom. One where my feet didn't touch the ground. One of escaping reality. Life became drugs, the intoxicating combination of dark sex addiction mixed with a never-ending supply of coke. I was a master of manipulation and game playing and always scored for free. I was locked in a prison of snow peaks and avalanches. I was determined to ski until all the snow on earth was gone. Oh lovely second eight ball.

Oh yes, another line or three. I always asked for more. It doesn't hurt to ask. I'll never get it if I don't. That cocaine rush gave me chills on my arms, goosebumps. I felt tense and blissful all at once. A good kind of crawling out of your skin. Sensual pleasure, over the top for me, was a given. Men on coke can't perform sexual intercourse, so you have to be more creative in the bedroom.

Via the phone line in the late morning after being up all night doing lots of drugs, I hooked up with Pablo, who promised he had lots of snow to share with his new bunny. He mentioned something about putting on women's panties. I ignored it because it grossed me out. I judged this person even before I met him. He came over; he wasn't my type, but I did a few lines. He bragged and asked me what every skier asked his bunny, "Isn't this good coke?"

I lied and said yes. Actually, it was really crappy coke, but I discovered that if I did enough of it, I could still get high. He wanted some stockings and a pair of panties. I decided to entertain him. The drug was flowing through my veins. Pablo went into the bathroom and came out looking like he was half a woman. He requested that I get into my own pair of stockings and fancy undies, so I did. Just before he had sex with me, I asked him, "Do you have any condoms?" He said no as we started having sex. I had broken another one of my rules of always having protected sex.

I started sleeping with more men from the party line, with men who sought prostitution. I would have sex with people I didn't even like or find attractive.

One night when I couldn't find drugs, I prostituted myself to a stranger from the phone line. I remember saying to myself, "Let's see how far I can go." It was unprotected sex and I had invited him directly into my home, without meeting him in public first. As a rookie, I did one thing "wrong" which could have saved me from addiction to prostitution. I didn't get the money upfront. So the guy walked off with the money and at 3 a.m. I was yelling after him down the stairwell to my building, "Come back here and GIVE ME MY MONEY!"

He said he'd be right back. Of course he was lying and was gone forever.

This was a new low. I was that whore my father always told me I was. I kept digging. I had not reached my bottom yet.

The next day, I got onto my Blackberry and searched on Craigslist. I responded to an ad that was looking for a ski bunny. I couldn't upload a photo, so I thought my chances were grim. I successfully seduced the guy with my words. We talked on the phone and he said, "Come on over."

I headed to Lincoln Park.

His place was up four flights of stairs with red carpet in the hallways. I didn't know what to expect, and was excited to go upstairs to find out. He met me at the door and escorted me to his room. He said he did not want to disturb his roommates. He laid out three lines for me and handed me a rolled up twenty–the green light to go. I eagerly did them.

I did not find David physically or emotionally attractive at all. But the fact that he was a high executive type who was also a drug dealer, was enough to more than peek my interest. It meant that the more I did for him, the more drugs he'd give me.

He informed me that someone would be over soon to pick up some drugs. Soon, there was a knock at the door. He brought a much older gentlemen into the room. As soon as the door closed they started making out. It startled me and did not turn me on. David, the drug dealer, was kissing a man who was super ugly and old. It was repulsive. They did some coke but there was no drug deal. I stayed to see what was going to happen next.

There was a second knock at the door. This time, a good-looking guy named Michael, came into David's room and bought himself a bag. David asked him if he wanted to have a party with us. Of course, he said, "Yes."

Michael did a few lines. I chimed in and snorted as much as I could–a big chunk of the mountain in front of us. Michael took his shirt off. The sexual kisses across the room with the drug dealer and the senior citizen didn't phase him. We started touching each other. This grew into erotic kisses. I told him I liked to be restrained, so we climbed onto the bed, he held me down. I could feel my heart beating out of my chest. Ten minutes later we were having sex with everyone watching.

I liked the attention.

Next on deck was a stockbroker in Downtown Chicago. There were cocaine crusties in my left nostril, and a metallic nasal drip. The minute

I laid my eyes on Kevin, I knew there was no attraction whatsoever. He lived in a beautiful place though. This guy was loaded! His cocaine was loaded too. Really good stuff. Amazingly good. We smoked cigarettes and realized we had nothing in common whatsoever. He wanted sex. I was higher than a kite in the sky. My entire body lit up. I didn't care who was going to touch me, as long as I could feed this ferocious addiction. I looked at his face, disgusted.

I went back to the living room afterward, so I could be close to the drugs. We both lit up cigarettes. He cut me off from the coke because I was doing too much. I threw a little fit, then went out on his balcony. We were 36 flights above the pavement of downtown Chicago. It was a small balcony with open spaces at your feet between the bars. I dipped my foot over the edge and saw how easy it would be to climb up and over the metal ledge. I thought to myself, "I could just jump and it will all be over."

At that moment, I felt a peaceful calm. I was scared of heights so I jumped back. That was God intervening. I went back inside and the ugly stockbroker wanted to have more sex. This time I said no. I left and went home. It was 6:30 a.m.

A few weeks later, I had a period of sobriety, just leaving a 12-step meeting. I walked to my car. My phone rang and I picked up without looking at the number. It was David, the drug dealer. He asked me how it's going and if I wanted to come over because he had some good coke.

I dropped recovery like a hot potato and quickly drove over there.

My heart was already beating fast. Post nasal drip had already begun. My mouth was watering, seething, I smiled at the endless supply that only a drug dealer can provide. I was not attracted to him in the least, but pretended to enjoy the sexual favors I did for him.

He told me that one of his friends was going to come over to have sex with me. He promised that his friend was good-looking. I waited nervously. He came in and was one of the ugliest men I'd ever set my eyes on. I watched him take off his clothes. I then wriggled out from underneath him Just in time. I told him that I was not having sex with that man.

David acted appalled and scolded me by telling me how rude I was being and that I better leave.

I drove home. It was 2:00 a.m. I was all coked up. I parked my car on Cicero in my neighborhood of Portage Park. I walked home.

The next day was my birthday. I felt like death warmed over. I walked to 7-11 for some American Spirit cigarettes. As I approached my car, I saw all the shattered windows and broken glasses. The thieves had stolen my laptop. It had 1/3 of a screenplay on the hard-drive and three years worth of writing–gone. The backup was in the laptop bag–gone too. The night before, when I was all coked up, I forgot to take my laptop to the safety of my apartment. Any valuables left in your car in the city of Chicago will most likely be stolen.

I started crying hard with the October sun beating down on me. I stopped crying to listen to a loud clear voice. God spoke loudly inside me. He said, "YOU ARE TAMPERING WITH YOUR LIFE. THIS IS ONLY A MATERIAL POSSESSION. THIS IS JUST A LAPTOP AND NOT YOUR LIFE. NOW, GET BACK INTO THE PROGRAM!"

I made a decision, right then and there, to put both my feet into the program. I told God that I'd do whatever it takes to stay clean.

Back from Relapse Prayer

Dearest Heavenly Father,

Shine light to help me get out of this place. I pray for the willingness to be willing to ask You and others for help. I have stumbled and tripped on my pride, on my ego. Thank You for the gift of desperation that made me "right-sized" and willing to ask for help.

The addiction brought me to my knees and the only direction, from here, is up. Show me Your Grace and move me out of paralyzing shame. Spark action into my cold bones. Get me moving in a healthy direction. You said I am your masterpiece. That I am your child. Protect me in your loving arms.

I am battered and bruised. My face was down in the mud for weeks. I have come up for air and the sun is shining. Jesus, wipe away my tears, the dirt from my eyes. Open my heart to feel your unconditional love. I was blind and now I beg you to heal my vision, to make me see life in a whole new way. To see potential and positive opportunities, connections and brightness in color. Let me feel your love in the hugs I will get from my fellows when I go back to my home group.

Protect me. You said that no weapon formed against me will prosper. What nearly destroyed me was stopped by Your Almighty Power. I was so lost and dim. Place me before my fellows to show me that I am not alone. I am powerless over all drugs of choice, and my life has become unmanageable. My life is in shambles. Devastation surrounds me like a war-torn landscape. I am coming to believe that You can lift me up out of my "self-will run riot," out of stubbornly doing it my way. Lift me out of trying to prove to myself that I can single-handedly get myself out alive and in one piece. The slippery slope of self-reliance leads to many falls.

Help me to lift up and wave the white flag of surrender to doing things Your Way. Give me direction and obedience to stay on track. Keep me focused as I journey through withdrawals–the shaking, the heat, the cold, the cravings, the triggers. Remove the disease of active addiction from the fabric of my being. Heal me. Guide me to do the next best indicated step.

Help me to stay close to you through the steps and principles of the program. My fellows are waiting for me with open arms. Lead me by the hand back to the 12-step rooms, where I am free to be myself. Where I can share how much I am hurting and I can hear victories, goals met, celebrations and sadness from the others. Be there in those rooms, working through the people. Be there while I feel my feelings that were frozen, like icicle tears never shed. Be there to catch me when I thaw out my vast array of colors of human emotions–Your Gifts that are so sacred, the inspiration of all forms of art. Grant me the ability to feel joy after feeling such agony. Keep me close to the rooms and assist me in building a broad foundation in which to build a strong recovery upon. Renew my hope. Keep me clean. I am now willing to do whatever it takes to stay sober. Show me the way.

In Jesus's Mighty Name.

Amen

* * *

Dearest Heavenly Father,

Shine light to help us get out of this place. We pray for the willingness to be willing to ask You and others for help. We have stumbled and tripped on our pride, on our ego. Thank You for the gift of desperation that made us "right-sized" and willing to ask for help.

The addiction brought us to our knees and the only direction, from here, is up. Show us Your Grace and move us out of paralyzing shame. Spark action into our cold bones. Get us moving in a healthy direction. You said we are your masterpiece. That we are your children. Protect us in your loving arms.

We are battered and bruised. Our faces were down in the mud for weeks. We have come up for air and the sun is shining. Jesus, wipe away our tears, the dirt from our eyes. Open our hearts to feel your unconditional love. We were blind and now we beg you to heal our vision, to make us see life in a whole new way. To see potential and positive opportunities, connections and brightness in color. Let us feel your love in the hugs we will get from our fellows when we go back to our home group.

Protect us. You said that no weapon formed against us will prosper. What nearly destroyed us was stopped by Your Almighty Power. We were so lost and dim. Place us before our fellows to show us that we are not alone. We are powerless over all drugs of choice, and our lives have become unmanageable. Our lives are in shambles. Devastation surrounds us like a war-town landscape. We are coming to believe that You can lift us up out of our "self-will run riot," out of stubbornly doing it our way. Lift us out of trying to prove to ourselves that we can single-handedly get ourselves out alive and in one piece. The slippery slope of self-reliance leads to many falls.

Help us to lift up and wave the white flag of surrender to doing things Your Way. Give us direction and obedience to stay on track. Keep us focused as we journey through withdrawals—the shaking, the heat, the cold, the cravings, the triggers. Remove the disease of active addiction from the fabric of our being. Heal us. Guide us to do the next best indicated step.

Help us to stay close to you through the steps and principles of the program. Our fellows are waiting for us with open arms. Lead us by the hand back to the 12-step rooms, where we are free to be ourselves. Where we can share how much we are hurting and we can hear victories, goals met, celebrations and sadness from the others. Be there in those rooms, working through the people. Be there while we feel our feelings that were frozen, like icicle tears never shed. Be there to catch us when we thaw out our vast array of colors of human emotions—Your Gifts that are so sacred, the inspiration of all forms of art. Grant us the ability to feel joy after feeling such agony. Keep us close to the rooms and assist us in building a broad foundation in which to build a strong recovery upon. Renew our hope. Keep us clean. We are now willing to do whatever it takes to stay sober. Show us the way.

In Jesus's Mighty Name.

Amen

Chapter 6:

House Cleaning
(Step 4)

**Step 4: Made a searching and fearless moral
inventory of ourselves.**

*He who is faithful in a very little thing
is faithful also in much; and he
Who is unrighteous in a very little thing
is unrighteous also in much.*
Luke 16:10 (NASB)

S tep 4 was a fact-finding mission. It didn't have to be an emotional
dysregulation, although identifying with feelings after a lifetime of
numbing was intense, especially those of resentment and fear. You
had to stay committed to your decision to turn over your life and will to
God and to be present with your feelings as they come up.

Feeling my emotions became a gateway for freedom. I had been on the
run most of my life, getting as far away or escaping how I felt about everything. The more I practiced tolerating uncomfortable feelings, whether

positive or negative, feeling them and identifying them, the less I wanted to act out. Numbing from feelings was what was at the core of my addictive behavior.

"You've got to feel them in order to heal them," said one wise program person I knew. Most of the time in early recovery, I didn't know what I was feeling. I had never practiced identifying feelings. I had just gone directly to numb-out mode. Any form of discomfort was immediately obliterated by using drugs. Actually, any emotion whatsoever, positive or negative, became a reason to use. I just didn't want to feel. Period.

One thing that helped me start identifying my feelings was a feelings wheel. It's a beautiful colored circle that has basic emotions in the center sections, with more specific and related emotions branching out. You can do a search on the internet for feelings wheel to find a variety of them. While utilizing one, I started to sense the basic emotions of either glad, sad or mad and then could explore exactly what was going on inside of me by listening to where I felt it in my body and acknowledging more specifics. Glad became happy, exuberant or satisfied. Mad became irritated, frustrated, furious or annoyed.

Another concept I learned in order to become more emotionally intelligent, was to make friends with my feelings. This sounded silly and corny at first, as well as a bit ridiculous. Emotions were anything but my friends. Emotions, however, are gifts from God. They are ways we can understand ourselves and the way we interact with the world and others. God gave us the full range of feelings so that we could fully live the human experience. If you numb one feeling, all of them are affected. If we allow ourselves to really feel what we are feeling, then we can experience the full range of emotions. Only good can follow—you start to be more in touch with your creativity. The burden and heaviness of unprocessed emotions inside your head is lifted. You begin to connect with others at a more authentic and deeper level. You begin to enjoy spending time alone with your Savior. You can tolerate being with yourself and in your own skin.

I began to learn more about feelings, the more I chose to feel them. Feelings are not facts and do not need to be acted on. Sometimes we feel old trauma being triggered. It does not mean it is representative of what is going on in the present. We feel the past and brace for the worst–the same storyline even though the past is over and the new storyline may be different. Something reminds us of what has already happened. PTSD is like a transparent blueprint placed over the present and we mix up the past with the present. We begin to FEEL what has already happened. I've learned this through learning how to manage Complex PTSD. Although not perfect, by a lot of self-reflection and hard work, I am able to navigate through my PTSD issues within hours or days instead of months on end.

We don't have to act out compulsive behavior just because we *feel* like doing it. We have choices. Acknowledging our feelings is vital to our wellbeing but checking them against reality is also very important. Just because you feel like drinking, doesn't mean you have to act on it.

Feelings won't kill you. It's the drugs and alcohol that will. I used to do this knee-jerk reaction to numb out with substances, because my feelings seemed too intense for me to tolerate them. Instead of feeling them, I avoided them and the fear inside me grew. This gave me the illusion that feeling my feelings was life threatening. Numbing them was a coping skill just to survive, just to get by.

When you're working on your fourth step, it's important to keep in mind that you have to feel in order to heal. Whatever you put your attention on, you are going to feel it. Remember the mantra when things get hairy "That was then, this is now."

The excavation of the soul is necessary as part of the recovery process. We uncover secrets. We unravel old resentments like dusty carpets. We shine light on our fears. We clean our houses and allow God to make the crooked lines straight.

Working a fourth step is about taking stock of what we have inside us. An inventory is taking pen to paper, filling the pages with our resentments, fears, character assets and sexual conduct. The Big Book describes it as doing inventory at a store. You can't really get a handle on what you've got until you've taken stock and documented it, so you can see a clearer picture of what you're dealing with. It's about getting organized and becoming honest enough to look yourself straight in the eye and write down what you see.

God showed me the way, through my sponsor and other fellows, to finish this important step, after I had lapsed during my first attempt. I could gain much strength from others who went before me as they openly and kindly shared their experience, strength and hope. All I had to do was ask. I couldn't do this alone.

I had to lean into Step 3. Into surrendering my strong emotions to God. I had to be sure to stay close to The Lord in all of this.

This was a massive fact-finding journey. A great spiritual housekeeping to free my soul, to clean up the messy life I was living and to take account-ability and responsibility for my part in things that happened, while I was an adult. I say this because as children we played no part in traumatic events—our young minds were still growing and we were vulnerable to the adults around us.

I stalled out and rested on my laurels several times in the middle of doing the fourth step. This is very dangerous and is a threat to your sobri-ety. It leaves all the unresolved resentments and character defects and fears floating around the surface, like open wounds, taunting you to go back to numbing instead of sticking with the painful feelings that come with the process of change. I just had to keep writing, putting one foot in front of the other, one baby step at a time, in order to finish the inventory. I was steadily finishing each section of the inventory moving closer to confes-sion and redemption in later steps.

One acronym for GOD is Good Orderly Direction. Throughout my recovery, I'd act like a teenager, rebellious and rejecting all suggestions given to me by my sponsor and resisting taking action when I knew it was the right thing to do.

I'd turn away from ideas that would improve my life and enhance my self-care. It was a typical case of "self-will run riot." What this means is that you try and control everything in life instead of accepting the way God is unfolding your life. You are trying to change people, places and things and you want things your way or the highway. The teenager within wants to take the easy way out. My inner teen wants what she wants when she wants it. And that's always NOW.

Self-care, adulting and self-improvement take effort and action. My inner teenager would avoid, numb or distract, in order to avoid taking positive action. I had to remind myself that feelings are not facts, I had to learn that this is a program of action and in order to get myself to take action I sometimes have to break down necessary actions, into bite-size baby steps and decide that "just for today" I can do what I know is the next best step to improve my life.

Releasing Resistance and Rebellion Prayer

God,

Hold my hand as I travel into the depths of recovery. Let me be open to learning from my mentors, my spiritual advisors and my sponsor. Lovingly and firmly shut my mouth so that I may listen and take bold action in faith.

Father God, I praise You for all the wealth, abundance, money, love and joy You have so freely given me in the past, present and into the future. Thank You for my ability to obey You. Thank You for my sponsor's wise presence in my life.

Release all rebellion, all resistance from the fabric of my being. I rest them at Your Feet for You to transform them, so I can better take care of myself and in turn, be of service to others. God, cast away doubts and build my confidence as I obey You more and more. Give me long term abstinence, one day at a time. Expand Your Grace inside me. Let me be open and willing to take suggestions during this fact-finding mission. Open my mind. Help me become a complete expression of Your Love. I give You my will and my life. I trust You and love You, Jesus. Improve my listening, my intuition, my ability to hear and act on guidance from The Holy Spirit working through my sponsor and others. Grow me up.

In Jesus's Mighty Name.

Amen

* * *

God,

Hold our hands as we travel into the depths of recovery. Let us be open to learning from our mentors, our spiritual advisors and our sponsors. Lovingly and firmly shut our mouths so that we may listen and take bold action in faith.

Father God, we praise You for all the wealth, abundance, money, love and joy You have so freely given us in the past, present and into the future. Thank You for our ability to obey You. Thank You for our sponsor's wise presence in our lives.

Release all rebellion, all resistance from the fabric of our beings. We rest them at Your Feet for You to transform them, so we can better take care of ourselves and in turn, be of service to others. God, cast away doubts and build our confidence as we obey You more and more. Give us long term abstinence, one day at a time. Expand Your Grace inside of us. Let us be open and willing to take suggestions during this fact-finding mission. Open our minds. Help us become a complete expression of Your Love. We give You our will and our lives. We trust You and love You, Jesus. Improve our listening, our intuition, our ability to hear and act on guidance from The Holy Spirit working through our sponsors and others. Grow us up.

In Jesus's Mighty Name.

Amen

The steps happen in the order they are in for a reason. A lot comes up in working Step 4. You must remember the decision you made to turn your will and life over to our Creator. The best way I can describe my experience is to lean into God. I had to lean in to stay close to Him. One of my sponsors believed that prayer and meditation were important tools to use from the beginning of working the program, to practice getting closer and closer to our Creator. He had me write a prayer at the top of each page of my fourth step. To start with a prayer. It kept me centered in God. It was like a surrender, an important connection with Him, a protection by His Grace, His Love. Some of these prayers were:

"Dear God, Let me stay present during this fact-finding mission."

"Dear Jesus, Keep me sober and focused as I work on Step 4."

Resentments were definitely not good news for addicts. If we held onto our bitterness we could not stay sober. It would eat away at us and the only "solution" or relief we would find is to drink over it. For years we have been drinking over the wrongs that have been done to us. Drinking over injustice. Drinking over anger. Drinking over our pride's rightness when everyone else was wrong. Drinking to celebrate. We failed miserably at our relationships, so we drank. We collected resentments that became a tangled mess, a web we did not know how to get out of without drinking, until now.

Untying the Knots of Resentment Prayer

Dear God,

Thank You for the sobriety and for the gift of surrender. I shall lean into You as I take this inventory, this great house cleaning. Let my pen keep on writing as I put resentment, fear, and sexual conduct down on paper. Keep me sober throughout this step—make it a safe place for me to untie the knots of resentment, to really explore what my part has been in matters, as an adult. Let me realize that all the trauma in my childhood was not my fault. I rest my will and my life and this work over to Your Peaceful Spirit. Help me stay spiritually fit as resentments surface. Let me feel my emotions rather than escape; lean into You instead of run away; connect with others and have conversations both in and out of the rooms with people who understand.

Thank You for the wonderful breakthroughs and self-awareness. Thank You for the capacity to be rigorously honest with myself, with my sponsor, with You, God. Help me as I straighten out these resentments, as I work through them and prepare to gain freedom from their tyranny. Thank You for the clear instructions of Step 4 to unleash and let go of what has fed my character defects. Purify me, God. Let me bravely move forward, and not rest on my laurels, during this important step. Give me the strength to keep going.

In Jesus's Mighty name I pray.

Amen

* * *

Dear God,

Thank You for the sobriety and for the gift of surrender. We shall lean into You as we take this inventory, this great house cleaning. Let our pens keep on writing as we put resentment, fear, and sexual conduct down on paper. Keep us sober throughout this step–make it a safe place for us to untie the knots of resentment, to really explore what our part has been in matters, as an adult. Let us realize that all the trauma in our childhood was not our fault. We rest our will and our life and this work over to Your Peaceful Spirit. Help us stay spiritually fit as resentments surface. Let us feel our feelings rather than escape; lean into You instead of run away; connect with others and have conversations both in and out of the rooms with people who understand.

Thank You for the wonderful breakthroughs and self-awareness. Thank You for the capacity to be rigorously honest with ourselves, with our sponsor, with You, God. Help us as we straighten out these resentments, as we work through them and prepare to gain freedom from their tyranny. Thank You for the clear instructions of Step 4 to unleash and let go of what has fed our character defects. Purify us, God. Let us bravely move forward and not rest on our laurels during this important step. Give us the strength to keep going.

In Jesus's Mighty name we pray.

Amen

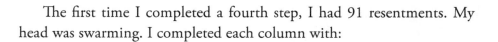

The first time I completed a fourth step, I had 91 resentments. My head was swarming. I completed each column with:

- The name of the person I harbored resentment against (don't forget yourself!)
- What happened (or what made me angry)?
- How did it affect me (my pocketbook, my self-esteem, my ambitions, my personal relationships)?
- What was my part in it?

Although it was uncomfortable writing about what happened and how it affected me (such as my self-esteem or pocketbook), the most challenging and humbling part was writing about my part in things. I found that the stronger the resentment, the harder it was to see that I played any role whatsoever in the matter. I closed my mind, crossed my arms and refused to acknowledge I had any part to play in the situation. That was the jumping off point of long and interesting discussions with my sponsor. Sometimes I was so locked into blaming the other person and/or into playing the victim, that there was just no WAY I had a part to play in what had happened. Always, upon further examination, there was something I had said or done, or assumed or expected, or not said or done, that contributed to the situation.

This excludes your childhood. The abuse you experienced was NOT YOUR FAULT. Your mind was still developing. You needed to be taken care of, guided, fed, nurtured and loved. If you did not get that, IT WAS NOT YOUR FAULT. End of story.

Another important exploration is examining your fears. Putting them down on paper. I had a lot of those too—and I found that my intense fears drove my behavior. I was usually hypervigilant from my nervous center being hijacked with the condition known as PTSD. This diagnosis was not an excuse, however, to not look my fears fully in the face. I was not a victim. I was a grown woman with choices.

I noticed that when I'm in a state of overwhelm, it becomes easy to feel unsafe and let my negative imagination go wild, thinking the worst possible outcomes will happen. Doing this has always made my heart beat faster. My energy then goes on high alert. It's part of the PTSD I experience. If I don't challenge the awful thoughts and imagery in my head, then a panic attack can easily manifest. Not feeling safe in a panicky state, I freeze and shut down. Sometimes, I am not able to calm down, the wheels of my mind are spinning out of control. My old solution was to go and do drugs to escape these strong feelings.

Today, that is not a solution. It is a ticket to hell. Now, when I let God into my problem, I can breathe again. I can, with His Help, slow down my energy and put my feet back down on the ground. I can see the possibility that I will get through it, without having to numb or escape the discomfort. Working the 12 steps has done wonders for my mental health. More importantly, so has my conscious relationship with God. I went from having debilitating PTSD episodes that would literally last weeks, sometimes months, to ones that last from a couple hours to a couple of days. I have also learned self-care through the 12 steps by using tools like reaching out to other members. All of this healing is made possible by the goodness of God. By Jesus's stripes I am healed. Sometimes quickly, sometimes slowly. It's in God's time and not in my time. I am so blessed that I have learned by the power of the 12 steps how to hand all things over to Christ and experience His Salvation in every corner of my life. God really *can* restore you to sanity.

Fear Inventory Prayer

Dear God,

Teach me how to stop being driven by fear. Grant me eagle's wings to live boldly. Let me thoroughly get my fears down on paper during this important inventory to take stock of what frightens me. While I do this, I hand over negative outlooks, where my fears run wild and I expect bad things. Put Your hedge of protection around me and infiltrate my mind with Your safety. Help me relinquish imagining the worst possible thing is going to happen. I surrender my low self-esteem and all forms of beating myself up, all shame and terror. God show me how to give myself some of Your Eternal Grace.

Give me the gift of living in the present. Show me how to be spiritually fit. Grant me the all-important powerful action to do Your Will. I want to be close to You, God. Teach me that being in Your Presence burns off fear. Let my fear inventory reveal how my fears are like ghosts of the past that cannot hurt me now. Help me stop believing the lie that it is only a matter of time before the other shoe drops. You said that no weapon formed against me will prosper. I praise You Lord, for Your Unwavering Safety and Protection.

Pull me closer to you. Show me how to be Your best friend, God. Animate my face with Your Bright Optimism. Let me be Your ambassador of love. Guide me to share my experience, strength and hope. Give me grace to inspire others and to be present with my love of humanity. I want to take the positive action to be of service to You and others, God. I am Yours. Do with me as Thou Wilt. Anoint me with Your gift of clear communication and compassion for myself and others. Sculpt me and change me into a better person. I love You, dear Lord. Match all my calamity with Your serenity.

In the name of Jesus,

Amen

* * *

Dear God,

Teach us how to stop being driven by fear. Grant us eagle's wings to live boldly. Let us thoroughly get our fears down on paper during this important inventory to take stock of what frightens us. While we do this, we hand over negative outlooks, where our fears run wild and we expect bad things. Put Your hedge of protection around us and infiltrate our minds with Your safety. Help us relinquish imagining the worst possible thing is going to happen. We surrender our low self-esteem and all forms of beating ourselves up, all shame and terror. God show us how to give ourselves some of Your Eternal Grace.

Give us the gift of living in the present. Show us how to be spiritually fit. Grant us the all-important powerful action to do Your Will. We want to be close to You, God. Teach us that being in Your Presence burns off fear. Let our fear inventory reveal how our fears are like ghosts of the past that cannot hurt us now. Help us stop believing the lie that it is only a matter of time before the other shoe drops. You said that no weapon formed against us will prosper. We praise You Lord, for Your Unwavering Safety and Protection.

Pull us closer to You. Show us how to be Your best friend, God. Animate our faces with Your Bright Optimism. Let us be Your ambassador of love. Guide us to share our experience, strength and hope. Give us grace to inspire others and to be present with our love of humanity. We want to take the positive action to be of service to You and others, God. We are Yours. Do with us as Thou Wilt. Anoint us with Your gift of clear communication and compassion for ourselves and others. Sculpt us and change us into better people. We love You, dear Lord. Match all our calamity with Your serenity.

In the name of Jesus,

Amen

Another thing that needed to be examined was my sexual conduct. Since I had too many lovers to count, my sponsor had me focus on those men I had relationships with or who stood out from the rest. I wrote about our relationships and what happened, what my part in it was in them ending; how I conducted myself. My pen became a time machine, tracing the letters, the sentences and paragraphs of everything that had happened, bringing it all to the surface for God to purify.

Many sponsors also had me list assets I had, qualities that served me as well as the world. This helped to counterbalance the negative excavation of digging up so much negativity from the past. After all this hard work, I was ready to do Step 5.

Chapter 7:

A Thorough Confession (Step 5)

```
Step 5: Admitted to God, to ourselves,
and to another human being the exact nature
of our wrongs.
```

Therefore, confess your sins to one another,
and pray for one another so
That you may be healed. The effective prayer
of a righteous man can accomplish much.
James 5:16 (NASB)

My sponsor often reminded me that our relationship was a trinity: it was her, me and Almighty God. All the details of the fourth step that rose to the surface, needed to be confessed to a trusted supportive human being and witnessed by God, Himself, as Step 5. I could feel God's presence there as I thoroughly and courageously confessed my resentments, one by one, reading the columns of my inventory across horizontally for the first time. It was emotional and freeing. I let the light of Jesus touch every fear that had ever tormented me. My sponsor gave me insight along the way. Pointed out patterns. Shared her experience, strength and hope. God's Holy Spirit was using them to speak to me. I felt like Step 5 was like putting down a sledgehammer and picking up a feather. I felt lighter and brighter as I let God and my sponsor show me the way.

The Gift of Confessions Prayer

Dear God,

I stand with You and my sponsor as the resentments stream down my face in tears. Grant me authentic power. Free me from pointing fingers of blame and being shackled to toxic injustice. Release me from a lifetime of self-centered righteousness. Show me that my confession is the beginning of being spiritually fit. Relieve me of the burden of carrying my shame and secrets. Plug me into Your Strength, Father God, to come before You with honesty, openness and willingness. Take away my fears. Show me Your Mercy. Replenish my soul with Your Truth. With You and my sponsor bearing witness, I can come clean of my wrongs.

Wash away my tears. Carry the debris of my past away and transform it into crystal clear clarity. Balance my emotions. Give me refreshment and a new way of life. Destroy the lies and lift the chains of secrecy and isolation. Show me how to trust You and to always take accountability for my actions.

Thank You for loving me through this process as I share my inventory with You and my sponsor. I praise You for giving me courage. Teach me how to embrace Your gift of change. Free my actions from bitterness and blame. Transform me into the person I am meant to become. With You, God, I am free to begin a new life.

In Jesus's Name I pray,

Amen

* * *

Dear God,

We stand with You and our sponsors as the resentments stream down our faces in tears. Grant us authentic power. Free us from pointing fingers of blame and being shackled to toxic injustice. Release us from a lifetime of self-centered righteousness. Show us that our confession is the beginning of being spiritually fit. Relieve us of the burden of carrying our shame and secrets. Plug us into Your Strength, Father God, to come before You with honesty, openness and willingness. Take away our fears. Show us Your Mercy. Replenish our souls with Your Truth. With You and our sponsors bearing witness, we can come clean of our wrongs.

Wash away our tears. Carry the debris of our past away and transform it into crystal clear clarity. Balance our emotions. Give us refreshment and a new way of life. Destroy the lies and lift the chains of secrecy and isolation. Show us how to trust You and to always take accountability for our actions.

Thank You for loving us through this process as we share our inventories with You and our sponsors. We praise You for giving us courage. Teach us how to embrace Your gift of change. Free our actions from bitterness and blame. Transform us into the people we are meant to become. With You, God, we are free to begin a new life.

In Jesus's Name I pray,

Amen

Loneliness follows an addict into the pits of despair. We think we are the only ones who are on the reckless road of active addiction. We stay away from others in fear of being different; judged harshly for having shame of a "lack of control." We internalize society's stigma of believing the lie that we are unforgivable bad people who are helpless, lost causes.

When we're sick in the disease, there is no time for connecting with others except to score a fix. Drug dealers and other users were part of the lifestyle. So was lying, manipulating and stealing to get our way. We hated ourselves.

Doing a fourth step inventory is a lot of work. It's a collection of reflective, honest and raw confessions. The fifth step is where we give it away, release all that has surfaced and trust another person with some of our deepest secrets.

Going over my fourth step inventory with my sponsor was deeply personal. Confessing my wrongs, resentments, and fears is a sacred vulnerable act. God bears witness to it. Our sponsor is the human being in whom we confide. We confess the development and the presence of fears and resentments that have ruled our lives for as long as we can remember. If we are honest with ourselves, there is great opportunity for freedom from the bondage of self. We have been on auto-pilot, driven by the toxic nature of resentments that led us deeper into the sickness.

Resentments are like taking poison and expecting the other person to die. Some are so deeply rooted that it takes meticulous examination of the workings of our minds, our thoughts, our emotions, our motives and our actions. Just as with every other aspect of recovery–we need help. We cannot do this on our own.

My first successful completion of a fourth step took me about three months. I literally had two journals filled with resentments, fears and my sexual conduct inventories.

It was a brisk and beautiful summer morning. I got a good night's sleep. I was nicely caffeinated and had eaten a healthy breakfast. I had my journals in hand, the pages filled with the ink of blood, sweat and tears. I had put pen to paper for almost three months straight, writing with brutal honesty, all that surfaced. I wanted to get better.

I left the house and took the short walk to the AA Clubhouse in the Congress Park neighborhood in Denver, Colorado. My sponsor had arranged for us to have the balcony on the second floor so we could talk and take cigarette breaks. We both had several unopened water bottles between us as well as three packs of Marlboro Reds. We were ready to take the journey of the fifth step together.

I was nervous and felt vulnerable. Being a deeply spiritual man, Derik A. spoke a prayer over me. I felt God's presence around us immediately. I felt God listening to me. I had exactly 99 resentments to go through. I opened up the first notebook and began to read my inventory out loud.

I started reading quickly, as if I just wanted to get it over with. My sponsor slowed me down, asking me questions to ponder and answer along the way. God took all the fear away from me and I became willing and open to listen to what my sponsor said. There was so much insight. I had a pen of a different color writing new notes that helped me sort out why I acted and reacted certain ways and how my past drove my behavior. Some of the questions and insight were hard to hear and challenging for me to answer. My sponsor was like a fresh, second pair of eyes looking at my life, noticing things I could not see because I was too close to it. I was unconscious of the patterns he pointed out. Like a silent attentive witness, I could feel God there with us the whole time, his compassion, forgiveness and love. My sponsor was being moved by God's Holy Spirit, guiding me to a better understanding of my life. It was so healing that light bulbs were going off in my brain; AHA moments left and right. I was moved to tears. I had never seen my life so clearly before.

After a couple hours, we took a break. We smoked cigarettes together on the porch, said hi to some of the other alcoholics there to attend a meeting or to do step work, and drank some gatorade from the café. While recognizing that my sponsor was human, with flaws and imperfections too, I had a lot of respect for him. My heart was filled with gratitude and appreciation for him taking time for me to take this important step. I learned from my past to not put any person on a pedestal. God and only God was on the throne. No human being.

We went back up to the balcony and picked up where we left off. The insight was astounding. Never in my life had I been given such transformational information in one sitting. Not in therapy or any other modality. It was just one alcoholic helping another. Simple as that.

The reason he could provide me with such insight was because he was a recovering addict, too. He had "been there." There are certain character traits that all addicts share. A commonality. Some of these were self-centeredness, self-reliance, dishonesty and selfishness, just to name a few.

We were on hour number four and had made a huge dent in doing my fifth step. We took another break. We stayed up on the balcony this time, listening to the birds in silence. I was wiping away the tears of releasing the toxic stubborn injustice I had harbored in the form of resentment my whole life. My emotions were being ironed out and it was nothing short of a miracle, plain and simple. I was taking more and more responsibility for my actions the more I shared my fourth step. In other words, I was growing up.

It took a total of six hours to complete my fifth step. I was totally exhausted and open and able to accept the celebratory words when my sponsor said, "That was a good job. Well done."

He gave me instructions before I went home. He asked me to read parts of the AA Big Book, review the steps I had done thus far to make sure that my work was thorough. I spend an hour in quiet solitude with my Creator.

Upon examining, I was really proud of my work thus far. I closed my eyes and rested in the presence of God. I felt like I had grown up from having the mind of a teenager to that of an adult.

The biggest take away was admitting to the self-centeredness from which I had operated my entire life. I unconsciously believed that the whole world revolved around me. I always, with no exceptions, took people's actions personally, as if what they said and did was a personal attack against me. It never occurred to me that they had their own stuff going on and I just happen to be around for them to express where they're at. Their behavior was about them more than it was about me.

I was very insecure and scrutinized myself constantly, kicking myself when I was down, criticizing myself endlessly. I believed the whole world could see right through me. I operated out of emotions and didn't realize that feelings are not always facts. I was stuck inside my own head, acting out of what dialectical behavioral therapy calls the emotional mind.

When a table full of strangers laughed out loud, I assumed they were all laughing at me. I thought every negative response that I witnessed from others was a direct reflection of me. I was super self-conscious, and to avoid the spotlight I so craved, I always pointed my finger, blaming others for my emotions, my choices, my actions, my spoken words.

So there was a lot of me, me, me. I was self-righteous, self-centered, selfish and self-reliant. I believed that I had to do things all by myself. I didn't trust anyone to "do the job for me" or to even help me, including God. I had to "prove to myself" that I could do it myself with nobody's help. Soon after entering into The Program, I came to realize it was a "we" program and not an "I" program. I could reach out; I could be a part of something greater than myself, I could relate to others and help them just as they helped me. We could get better together.

Years later, in my sex addiction program, I took my first sponsee through her fifth step.

It was another warm summer day. I had scoped out a big café in Littleton that had tiny rooms available to rent. There was a small table and two chairs in each room. We arranged our iced teas and water bottles for the long work ahead. I went into the room. Journals in hand, my sponsee followed. I closed the door, closing the rest of the world out. It was a trinity—me, her and God present. I said a prayer over us and she began reading me her fourth step. God revealed patterns in her emotional response to life. I took notes and then went through them when I felt God moved me to speak. She took notes and I could sense light bulbs going off in her mind, the same way that light bulbs had turned on during my fifth step.

She was going through the hurt and resentment of some of her family members and she started crying. The tears kept coming. I watched her face. I did not interrupt her crying. I just watched and listened. I stared at a big tear rolling down her face and I thought to myself, "this is what it means to be human."

My sponsee's old tears and hurt were coming up and out for God to touch them with His Sunlight of the Spirit. It was like God was hugging her and comforting her in His embrace. I touched her hand and she cried even harder. I cried with her.

So much was coming up. I shared my insight after she had stopped crying. I shared that this was a great opportunity for her to take responsibility for her part in things (when she was an adult).

God was there in the air. He was with both of us in that little room. There was a stillness. The words that came out of my mouth were not completely mine, it seemed, but were guided by God's Holy Spirit. There were bold realizations, subtle ones, loud glaring ones. All this was in the spirit of releasing what no longer served her. It wasn't about changing her. It was about bringing her awareness to patterns that I could see. As she was reading the last part of her inventory, I closed my eyes and saw a flock of blue birds taking flight. She was free.

We looked at each other in silence and both smiled at the same time. She felt it too. She felt freedom from the bondage of self. She experienced the fifth step promises, same as I had after doing my fifth step. These are written in the AA Big Book:

"We pocket our pride and go to it, illuminating every twist of character, every dark cranny of the past. Once we have taken this step, withholding nothing, we are delighted. We can look the world in the eye. We can be alone at perfect peace and ease. Our fears fall from us. We begin to feel the nearness of our Creator. We may have had certain spiritual beliefs, but now we begin to have a spiritual experience. The feeling that the drink problem has disappeared will often come strongly. We feel we are on the Broad Highway, walking hand in hand with the Spirit of the Universe."

It was on to Step 6.

Chapter 8:

Humility and Willingness to Surrender Our Wrongs (Steps 6 and 7)

Step 6: Were entirely ready to have God remove all these defects of character.

Step 7: Humbly asked God to remove our shortcomings.

Humble yourselves in the presence of the Lord,
and He will exalt you.
James 4:10 (NASB)

S ometimes we take pleasure in being mean, angry or acting superior, dramatic, intense, controlling or in seeking attention, whether positive or negative. It feels good to feel better than someone else or to blow off some steam. It's easier to act out of a negative place, out of habit–than to challenge them.

In our disease we were liars, manipulators, deceivers, thieves. Control freaks. We wanted what we wanted when we wanted it and we wanted it now. The addiction really wreaked havoc on our personalities.

Character defects are like broken parts of our personality that formed as a result of learning them as children and not changing them as adults. They were often survival skills, as ways to cope with a dysfunctional situation. We continue to use these survival skills that no longer serve us. Character defects are parts of the personality that create problems in our lives and relationships. Some examples range from being dishonest, selfish, slothful, being gluttonous to being controlling, self-centered and attention-seeking, being lazy, self-reliant (vs. being reliant on God), argumentative and pessimistic. Character defects support the disease of addiction.

Character defects, or shortcomings, are not based on love, compassion or acceptance. Having character defects is part of being human—so there's no shame. It's part of the human condition. Step 6 along with 7 gives us the opportunity to give these up and really propel personal change. Working these steps provides an opportunity to gain freedom from those parts of our personality that did not serve the world. Only with God's help, of course.

My selfishness, self-centeredness, gluttony, sloth, pride and many other character defects became apparent to me in the excavation of my soul while working Steps 4 and 5. During the challenging but necessary inventory, and through giving away my Step 5 to my sponsor and God I saw many more glaring character defects. I became willing to have The Lord transform me, so every part of my being was ready for this surrender. Then I humbly asked God to remove all my shortcomings, as done in Step 7. It is only by God's grace that I was saved. Only He can remove what no longer served me.

I feared letting go of the defects of character that have been survival skills throughout the span of my life. My willingness to be ready to surrender took work and was a testimony of my growth in the program.

Make Me Ready Prayer

Dear God,

Make me ready to do Your Will. Keep me moving forward. Prevent me from turning back or giving up. I pray for the willingness to be willing to surrender my character defects to You. Father God, guide me with Your wisdom through Your Holy Spirit, so that I see that my shortcomings are harmful to my soul and damaging to my recovery and my relationships to others. Let me accept my humanity. Help me understand that my growth and change are about progress not perfection. Put me in touch with my assets and let them grow strong roots as I become more compassionate, patient, kind and loving. Relieve me of the compulsion to entertain ideas of plotting and planning to use all my drugs of choice. I'm going to follow You into Your Brilliant Love. Jesus, I accept Your Salvation. Teach me how to forgive myself as You have forgiven me. Help me rest in Your Peace and Tranquility. Show me how to be gentle with myself and to know that things are done on Your Watch, God, and not mine. Help me to be patient in knowing that some things take time. I pray for the willingness to be willing to let You shape me and transform me into the best version of myself. Position me to live an honest life, free of the character defects that used to give me pleasure. Give me many beautiful opportunities to be of service to others. Help me to make a positive impact on the people around me. Embrace me in Your Comfort. Help me grieve the loss of all past brokenness. Steady me for You to remove all harmful behaviors from the fiber of my being. Keep me sober while doing it. Love me until I can love myself. Chisel away the self-centeredness, selfishness, dishonesty, self-reliance, resentment, anger and pride. Let me trust that You are in the driver's seat. I pray for the willingness to let go and have faith that there is a better way of living on the horizon. Help me to let go and have You do with me as Thou Wilt.

In Jesus's name I pray.

Amen

* * *

Dear God,

Make us ready to do Your Will. Keep us moving forward. Prevent us from turning back or giving up. We pray for the willingness to be willing to surrender our character defects to You. Father God, guide us with Your wisdom through Your Holy Spirit, so that we see that our shortcomings are harmful to our soul and damaging to our recovery and our relationships to others. Let us accept our humanity. Help us understand that our growth and change are about progress not perfection. Put us in touch with our assets and let them grow strong roots as we become more compassionate, patient, kind and loving. Relieve us of the compulsion to entertain ideas of plotting and planning to use all our drugs of choice. We're going to follow You into Your Brilliant Love. Jesus, we accept Your Salvation. Teach us how to forgive ourselves as You have forgiven us. Help us rest in Your Peace and Tranquility. Show us how to be gentle with ourselves and to know that things are done on Your Watch, God, and not on ours. Help us to be patient in knowing that some things take time. We pray for the willingness to be willing to let You shape us and transform us into the best versions of ourselves. Position us to live an honest life, free of the character defects that used to give us pleasure. Give us many beautiful opportunities to be of service to others. Help us to make a positive impact on people around us. Embrace us in Your Comfort. Help us grieve the loss of all past brokenness. Steady us for You to remove all harmful behaviors from the fiber of our beings. Keep us sober while doing it. Love us until we can love ourselves. Chisel away the self-centeredness, selfishness, dishonesty, self-reliance, resentment, anger and pride. Let us trust that You are in the driver's seat. We pray for the willingness to let go and have faith that there is a better way of living on the horizon. Help us to let go and have You do with us as Thou Wilt.

In Jesus's name I pray.

Amen

Words are cheap. You can say you are ready, but your words may not necessarily be backed up by action. Your heart and mind must be ready to change.

Steps 6 and 7 are about willingness and humility. They are about preparing, becoming ready to ask God to remove your character defects and then, with a willing and humble heart, asking Him to remove them.

Being entirely ready to give up something that has served you in some way, involves communication with yourself and with God. A lot of meditation, reflection, writing and soul searching. Talking it out with your sponsor and other fellows in the program or trusted friends helps too. It is not only making that decision to have God transform you with the removal of your defects, but actually placing them up to God to take now or later, as He Will in His Time.

Being entirely ready is felt wholeheartedly and takes courage. It is not merely an intellectual matter. It involves the faith that when God takes what no longer serves you or the rest of humanity, that you trust Him to mold and shape you like a slab of clay on the potter's wheel, in order for you to be of better service to yourself, and to the world. Working a Step 7 is like unknotting the mind. It explores the pros and cons of keeping character defects vs. giving them up. I really had to reflect on my own willingness to explore new territory. It meant that I had to learn to cope with reality in healthier ways. Steps 6 and 7 make a way to let go of addictive thinking, to thrive and bring service and love to others. In order for me to make way for the new, I had to be willing to let go of the old and allow

God to transform me entirely, or to be as ready as I could at the stage of life when doing a Step 7. Remember this is about progress, not perfection.

The first time I went through Steps 6 and 7, it was done very quickly. I was told that this was "the AA way." That is, immediately following my fifth step confession, I was told to go home, and spend an hour with God. Just me and Him. I reviewed the previous steps I had taken (Steps 1-5). Reading the steps out loud from the AA Big Book to see if I had done them thoroughly and to the best of my ability. I then gathered the list of character defects I had identified throughout my inventory (Step 4) and through the feedback I had received from my sponsor (during Step 5). I looked at each one thoughtfully, asking myself if I was able to give them up to God. The ones that I didn't were ones that were some of my oldest survival skills or defense mechanisms that helped me get by in life. Because they were so ingrained, they were harder for me to let go of. So, I asked God for the willingness to be willing to give these character defects to Him, since right now I did not feel I had that willingness. I had so many of them and was not willing to give up most of them. I prayed the seventh step prayer over and over again, each time substituting the words "character defects" with the specific one I was working on. I literally had dozens.

Here is the Seventh Step Prayer:

> My Creator,
> I am now willing that you should have all of me, good and bad. I pray that you now remove every single defect of character that stands in the way of my usefulness to You and my fellows. Grant me strength as I go out from here, to do your bidding.
> Amen

So, for instance, I would address my self-centeredness and cater the prayer to that specific character defect, praying:

"...I pray that you now remove the *self-centeredness* that stands in the way of my usefulness to You and my fellows..."

Afterward, I felt lighter, I felt there was hope of a possibility of changing my ways, a possibility of giving up those things that no longer served me; to trust God with my life. To let go of control and give it to Him instead.

In other 12-step programs, Steps 6 and 7 are worked in different and various ways—mostly there is more time for reading about each step and to do reflective writing in answering some very poignant questions, such as: Why don't I want to give this character defect up? What am I getting out of this characteristic? What do the character defects do *for* me? What do they do *to* me?

These two steps are very enlightening because you are digging into your character in an honest, down to earth and humble way. You are deepening the exploration of what makes you tick and determining if those things are healthy or not. And ultimately, there is a deepening of faith to let God in and do with your character defects as He Will.

I had pages of character defects when I first went through these steps. Miraculously, God has since removed many of them. Some of them have disappeared completely–out of sight, out of mind. Completely removed from my personality. Some of them still exist as thoughts that pop up, but God granted me keen awareness of making a choice to act out the character defect or not, and I simply decide to not do it by doing the opposite action instead. I do not bring that characteristic back to life through my words or actions. I have learned to leave the character defect dormant in thought-form only; to keep taking the power out of it by not acting on it. To take positive action instead.

Speaking of positives, we cannot look at character defects without looking at the flipsides–our assets. It's important work to recognize those parts of yourself that are nurturing and bring good into the world. The best sponsors I've had will have me also explore my character assets and write about them, bring them to mind and to recognize my own inherent goodness.

It took some brainstorming to dig up assets but once I got going, God put the words in my head. Some of the assets I had were seemingly opposite of the character defects. That's how complicated or human we are—we can have two seemingly opposite qualities, or dialectics, co-existing inside of us.

Some of my assets I discovered with pen and paper included kindness, being loving, positive, friendly, trustworthy, social, purposeful, disciplined (in some areas), creative, courageous, clean, optimistic, faithful, candid, confident, inspiring, cooperative, hard working, open-minded, smart, expressive, confidential, has integrity, supportive, intuitive, generous, etc.

A lot of these asset qualities were simply the other side of the coin of the defects. For instance, if you address dishonesty by working Steps 6 and 7, you become honest. If you allow God to have your hostility, then that makes room for some of its opposites—kindness, understanding, patience.

I am not only a recovering addict myself, but I work with other addicts in early recovery at my day job as a Peer Specialist at a mental health center. One thing I've noticed is that the most determined and driven people in the world are those who were once locked in the jaws of addiction and are now recovering addicts, healing one day at a time. They used to have razor-sharp focus, using every ounce of their energy toward getting their drug of choice. Once in recovery they can harness that same energy, allowing God to transform it into an asset to accomplish whatever they set their minds to do. It's extraordinary. Many recovering addicts become successful business owners, non-profit start-ups, dancers, entertainers, CEOs, thought leaders, angel inventors and philanthropists. All once down and out in the crux of active addiction. Now not taking anything for granted, humbly working a program of recovery and using that razor-sharp focus and drive to create a life they love through their openness, willingness and honesty.

Humility is the cornerstone of Step 7. One definition I love of humility is **freedom from pride or arrogance**: the quality or state of being humble. My concept of humility is having both feet on the ground, acknowledging God in my life and staying true and close to who I truly am. It means staying out of my character defects and being ego-driven or feeling superior. It is about being grateful for what I have and appreciating and respecting those around me. Being receptive to be of service and taking that action on a regular basis.

In Step 6, we worked on becoming entirely ready. During Step 7, we ask God to take our character defects. The seventh step required faith, trust, and the willingness that we developed during Step 6. It is going to God and asking for help. It is humbling to ask for help.

Humility to Let Go and Let God Prayer

Dear Jesus,

Grant me humility. Release me from grandiosity, negative judgment and arrogance. Let me follow Your lead without stepping on my own toes; without trying to run the show. Reveal my purpose and give me the strength to carry it out. Guide me and open my mind to listen and act on the suggestions of my sponsor. Give me the insight to place every situation into Your hands and allow me to realize I cannot change by myself; that I need Your help. Give me the eyes to see the things that I can change and the wisdom that I am powerless over other people, places and things.

Help me stay free of addictive patterns, from obsessions. I know I am not perfect, God. I am ready to have You change my life and remove all the defects of character that prevent me from being of service to You and others. Transform my life. Make me Your trusted servant. Make me aware that I can rest in the peace of the loving comfort You wrap me in. I just need to tune in to it to feel it. I am Your loving child. Protect me and all those I interact with today. Remove all the character defects that prevent me from doing Your Will. Show me the gifts and assets You have given me and let me act on them. Thank You for another day of sobriety.

In Jesus's Name.

Amen

* * *

Dear Jesus,

Grant us humility. Release us from grandiosity, negative judgment and arrogance. Let us follow Your lead without stepping on our own toes; without trying to run the show. Reveal our purpose and give us the strength to carry it out. Guide us and open our minds to listen and act on the suggestions of our sponsors. Give us the insight to place every situation into Your hands and allow us to realize we cannot change by ourselves; that we need your help. Give us the eyes to see the things that we can change and the wisdom that we are powerless over other people, places and things.

Help us stay free of addictive patterns, from obsessions. We know we are not perfect, God. We are ready to have You change our life and remove all the defects of character that prevent us from being of service to You and others. Transform our lives. Make us Your trusted servants. Make us aware that we can rest in the peace of the loving comfort you wrap us in. We just need to tune in to it to feel it. We are Your loving children. Protect us and all those we interact with today. Remove all the character defects that prevent us from doing Your Will. Show us the gifts and assets You have given us and let us act on them. Thank You for another day of sobriety.

In Jesus's Name.

Amen

Addicts who are lost in their disease don't ask for help because we think that we have to do everything by ourselves. This is the limitation of self-reliance. We feel self-hatred and shame for what we do and we truly believe we are all alone and that nobody can help us. We underestimate the miracles that God can perform in our lives. We all need help to recover from the "cunning, powerful and baffling" disease of addiction from God and others in the program. God is the answer to all my problems just as importantly as acceptance.

After we humbly ask God to remove our shortcomings, we leave the results up to Him and continue praying for the willingness to give away all of our defects; to let go of the grip we once had on them and to Let Go and Let God. God wants and knows what is best for us. He will meet our efforts with miracles. As they say in the ninth step promises "You will be amazed before you are halfway through."

It's a promise. It works if you work it. The 12 steps are an incredible design for living that is deeply transformational; so full of the richness of fellowship and camaraderie; full of gifts around every corner. I have, at times, thanked God for making me a recovering addict because without crossing paths with the 12 steps, I don't know where I would be in my own development as a growing human being. These 12 steps not only saved my life but have provided me with a high quality of life that have brought me into a loving and conscious relationship with God, my Creator. Totally priceless.

Chapter 9:

Making Wrongs Right (Steps 8 and 9)

Step 8: Made a list of all persons we have harmed
and became willing to make amends to them all.

Step 9: Made direct amends to such people
whenever possible, except when to do so would
injure them or others.

The Lord has commanded to do as has been done this day,
to make atonement on your behalf.
Leviticus 8:34 (NASB)

A fter my Step 4 inventory revealed who I had harmed, writing my actual eighth step list was a piece of cake. My willingness was not as solid as making that list. I started becoming anxious; started speculating how people might react to the amends, even before they were written. Was I going to mend relationships? Will the person I am giving amends to yell at me? Reject me? Abandon me? Hate me? Spit in my face?

Will they want nothing to do with me? Suddenly fear of the "what ifs" were in the driver's seat.

Addiction wreaks havoc on all relationships including the one we have with ourselves and with God. It isolates the addict. I was not present. I only had my eyes open to how and when I would get the next fix. I generally lied to myself and others about the seriousness of my active addiction problem.

My willingness to make my Step 8 list came into focus when I saw my part in things in Step 4 and shared them with my sponsor and God in Step 5. I became willing and ready to put the character defects that were at play into God's Mighty Hands, asking that He remove them in His time. I didn't want to leave any stone unturned. I wanted to be thorough and my willingness to make things right became solidified in my Step 8 list.

Step 8 is constructing a list of people you have harmed. It was not so daunting now that I got those people's names down on paper.

This step was also about asking God for the willingness to make amends to each person on the list, even if I didn't really want to. Sometimes that willingness took time to develop. I used a lot of prayer and meditation during this step. Gathered courage and faith to develop the willingness to make the amends to everyone on that list. I remember contemplating and gauging my willingness to see if I was ready. If there was still justified anger or flickers of resentment, I might have to go back to my fourth step and explore what my part was in what happened—and to possibly add to it. I also had to sometimes pray for the willingness to be willing to make the amends.

Step 8 was the beginning of prep work in a vigorous attempt at making wrongs right. In an SA book called *Step Into Action,* it says that "righting our wrongs becomes the single most powerful tool for success in spiritual growth and recovery. Why? It gets the wrongs out of the way so God can work in us…"

Forgiveness is required. If we don't foster forgiveness, then we can easily point the finger of blame toward the person we suspect we need to make an amend to. This happened especially if the person wronged me first. I held on to "justified anger" or bitter resentment that felt as though it wouldn't budge. It created a stuck feeling; a refusal to see my part in things.

We can be inspired by God's Word and embrace forgiveness with the inspiration of how God so thoroughly forgives us.

EPHESIANS 4:32 (NLT) reads
"Instead be kind to each other and tenderhearted, forgiving one another just as God through Christ has forgiven you."

Now is a great time to turn to God, to pray for the willingness to be willing to forgive those you have wronged in addition to forgiving yourself. Your name should be on that list of amends, too. After all, in our active addiction, we really did hurt ourselves. We neglected ourselves and were in a state of spiritual bankruptcy. I took self-destructive actions that put my life in harm's way. I neglected the basics—not drinking adequate amounts of water, not eating healthy, my sleep was sporadic and self care was practically non-existent.

Willingness to Make Amends Prayer

Dear God,

Guide my hand as I make my eighth step list of those I have harmed. Let it be thorough and honest. Bring me courage to write the names of the people I have harmed down on paper. Grow my willingness to be willing to make my amends. Grant me patience with myself and tenderness toward my own humanity. Teach me self-love and acceptance. Grant me clarity. Grow compassion toward those I have hurt. Take away all expectations. Teach me how to listen to You with my heart and soul. I want to do Your Will, God. I know that I must do this important work so I can better serve you in expanding

Your Kingdom. To experience freedom from the turmoil of hurting others throughout the span of my life.

The resentments I have clung onto are being set free like butterflies from a net. There is unfinished business, for I need to take accountability for my part in the resentments that I have stubbornly held onto for days, weeks, months, years, even decades. I know with Your Help, Jesus, I can do this. I am willing to seek Your Counsel. Warm my heart with Your Grace weaved into all my endeavors. Make my list thorough. Grant me inspiration from those who have gone before me, to get ready, to be more and more willing with each passing day. Give me a brave heart and freedom from self-will. I lay all the shame and worry and depression at your feet as I prepare for unknown results of the list I am about to act on. Set me on the right path and keep me safe in recovery while I make this important list and get ready to make my amends.

In Jesus's name,

Amen

* * *

Dear God,

Guide our hands as we make our eighth step lists of those we have harmed. Let it be thorough and honest. Bring us courage to write the names of the people we have harmed down on paper. Grow our willingness to be willing to make our amends. Grant us patience with ourselves and tenderness toward our own humanity. Teach us self-love and acceptance. Grant us clarity. Grow compassion toward those we have hurt. Take away all expectations. Teach us how to listen to You with our hearts and souls. We want to do Your Will, God. We know that we must do this important work so we can better serve You in expanding Your Kingdom. To experience freedom from the turmoil of hurting others throughout the span of our lives.

The resentments we have clung onto are being set free like butterflies from a net. There is unfinished business, for we need to take accountability for our part in the resentments that we have stubbornly held onto for days, weeks, months, years, even decades. We know that with Your Help, Jesus, we can do this. We are willing to seek Your Counsel. Warm our hearts with Your Grace weaved into all our endeavors. Make our lists thorough. Grant us inspiration from those who have gone before us, to get ready, to be more and more willing with each passing day. Give us brave hearts and freedom from self-will. We lay all the shame and worry and depression at your feet as we prepare for unknown results of the list we are about to act on. Set us on the right path and keep us safe in recovery while we make this important list and get ready to make our amends.

In Jesus's name we pray.

Amen

Making Amends

My sponsor and I would meet at Starbucks once a week to "hammer out" my amends, one by one. We spent a lot of time talking about how I felt about situations that came out of my fourth step and went from the biggest, most accessible people, along with the biggest resentments to work on first. My number one resentment I had was toward my father.

My dad was violent when I was growing up and very cruel to me. As a four-member family unit, it was me, my brother and mom who were always anxiously waiting in fear the closer the time came to my father coming home from work.

My childhood and teenage life was like walking through a minefield—never knowing when a bomb was going to blow up in my face. There was danger in the air most of the time. As a young sixth-grade kiddo, I remember being so super self-conscious of myself, of the way I swung my arms and feeling/believing that everyone was watching me, laughing and criticizing the way I held my body, the way that I moved.

My mom always told me to "just smile," and that smiling would get you through anything. I was told to smile big. When my two best friends arrived on a yellow school bus, I was feeling especially low, as there was a big blowout at my parents' house the night before. All I could hear myself say was "Smile big." I unnaturally smiled as big as I could after the bus arrived and my friends stepped off. They both laughed and asked me why I was smiling so strangely. I was so hurt by this comment and their laughter. I practiced smiling smaller to avoid being made fun of. I was a confused and beat up kiddo.

On the playground, I was my own worst critic. I condemned myself and drowned in waves of fear and shame. I was left feeling completely caved in, defeated in my heart by my father's hurtful words and hitting and pinching and being physically and emotionally abusive to my mother. It was really hard to grow up with this. I remember one time I witnessed my father taking a whole gallon of milk, pouring it onto the kitchen floor, throwing a rag in my mom's face and telling her to clean it up.

Helpless, Hopeless Confusion

What made my childhood even more confusing is that I knew my dad loved me. He strangely was the person I connected to more than anyone else in my immediate family. The older I got, the more I discovered I was one pissed off teen. I slapped my friend's face once over a petty misunder-standing. Then once, when being attacked by a skinhead girl, I hit her on the side with a stolen skateboard with all my might and she fell and rolled down a grassy hill of a high school campus. Both me and my best friend ran the opposite way with all our might.

As an adult, I looked at an old photograph taken when I was in pre-school—I was holding a foam ball—and I saw so much sadness, fear and emotional pain in my eyes. At my parents', it was loud, but to the outside world, things looked "perfect." My father was a narcissist who had undiagnosed and untreated mental illness. I believe he had bipolar as well, bipolar II.

I put a lot of thought into my amends. I made sure to take accountability for my part in things. I admitted my wrongs along with expressing and committing to actions of what I was going to do and how I was going to make the wrong, right.

My first amend was to my dad. I remember sweating, my heart beating fast as I drove to the suburbs to pick him up. Through doing this amend thoroughly with the help of God and my sponsor, I was prepared to tell my father that I had blamed him for everything wrong in my life as an adult and that I intended to take responsibility for my life and to stop blaming him from now on. There were other things in that amend, too.

We sat on a park bench in the warm sunshine overlooking a field of big trees with the sound of birds on a warm day. Shaking, I took a deep breath and read him the amend, straight from my index card.

"I'm a sex addict. I'm in a program of recovery. I won't recover unless I clean up my past. I owe you an amend. I disrespected you by lying to you constantly. I've blamed you for everything. I've acted ungrateful and demanding. I overreacted. I humiliated you by verbally abusing you. I tried to control you. I acted self-centered and entitled.

"I am willing to do whatever it takes to make things right.

"My amend to you is to be honest. I will take responsibility for my life. I will treat you with respect. I will respond rather than react. I will take your feelings into consideration. I will no longer try to control you.

"Have I left anything out?"

Then I zipped my lip to let him speak if he wanted to say something. He talked for an hour and a half and confided in me and told me that he loved me. That was the day we became friends, seven years before he died of bone cancer. When he died, there were no resentments and no regrets. An absolute miracle in my life. Only by the grace of God. In the end, there was only love.

After a meeting during some fellowship with a fellow, I told him that after I gave my amend to my father, I felt like an adult now and that it somehow grew me up. He said, "That's because you did grow up."

It was nice to be validated! We both laughed together at the obviousness of it.

While working Step 9, I had so many spiritual awakenings, and so much shifted for me. I started feeling the peace of Jesus in my heart. God was showing me now how to flow with life on life's terms–life the way it naturally unfolded–the victories, challenges–the whole gamut. At times, especially after the amends I made with my immediate family, I felt like I was flying high like an eagle, clean as a whistle. I let go of so much and walked through the fear of how others would respond to my attempts to make amends for the harm I had done.

While doing my amends, both big and small, some did not come out favorably. Some old friends I had wronged did not have anything to do with me, and my attempts to make amends were met with dead silence. So I sent them letters and grieved the losses. My ex-husband canceled meeting with me twice. I really wanted to express and take responsibility for the damage I had caused in the wreckage of our four-year marriage. I discovered during the course when I wrote up living amends, that I had harbored a hope that we would become friends. That was not in the cards, and would have created more problems. I didn't get what I wanted. I had to really lean into God during these times, and trust Him, that some things were not meant to be the way I wanted them to be.

Living amends are really powerful. They were thought out, written down and carried out. Faith without works is dead. You had to back them up with action. They were amends you were making in your life to change the pattern of how you conducted yourself from this point forward. One example was with my ex-husband. Some of the living amends I made was to have healthy and clear dialogue with romantic partners, rather than yelling and abusing them, out of a desperation to try and control them. I made a commitment to not make a man the center of my world, but to have a healthy partnership in which we both have independent lives doing hobbies, having friends and having interests that might not always be in alignment with the other person and accepting that reality. I made living amends to be kind to men and not to use my tongue as a weapon. I was good at this. I hurt a lot of people with my sharp tongue and creative, verbally abusive words. I made good on the wrongs, even when I couldn't involve the other person. It made me a better person, going through the pain of things not panning out my way. Acceptance really is the answer to all my problems. It's not always easy to take responsibility for your actions. As a matter of fact, it can be quite humbling. And to make a solid commitment to change often felt like a nearly impossible mission. But it can be done and the dividends are quite generous and in your favor.

I was enlightened and doing God's will more and more. I was taking action. I was feeling the fear and doing it anyway, and eventually, overall, the fear faded into the background of my existence. It did not disappear completely but was no longer in the foreground.

All the famous AA 9th Step Promises came true for me while making my powerful, and sometimes scary amends. I no longer regretted the past. I experienced true serenity and peace. My selfishness disappeared. No longer was I afraid of facing people or my finances. "No matter how far down the scale we have gone, we will see how our experience can benefit others."

That one really hit home and showed me that all my pain was not in vain. It was to help others in their own recovery from addiction.

God was doing for me what I could not do for myself. I could reflect on situations and see how, when I relied on Jesus Christ, I didn't have to carry the burden of trying to figure things out myself. God already did that for me. All I need to do is lean on Him, take responsibility for my actions and stay humble and open to learning and growing.

I now recognized how God is constantly helping, guiding, loving and supporting me.

The promises all came into more focus, the more amends I made. Every single one. I am living proof and if they can come true for me, they can come true for you too. All in God's timing–sometimes quickly, sometimes slowly. Be patient with yourself.

Taking Responsibility Prayer

Dear God,

I lean into the third step as I work through the task of placing my heart and mind onto the table to make my amends. I turn my will and my life over to You, God. Let this reassure me that things will turn out the way they are meant to be. Let me be thorough in this process. Hold my hand, Jesus–let me be guided by Your Everlasting Love. Grace me with the awareness of feeling Your love for me. That the results are in Your hands and all I need to do is let go of control. Let my intentions be pure, to make right what I have wronged. Help me to take accountability for my life. Grow me up. Guide me to find the right words and to delay–to keep going. Grant me spiritual experiences as I do my amends and I trust the process of how others will respond and to accept and invite You into the fire if the results are not what I want. Let me accept and respect those who I have harmed. For I have grown ever expansive faith in living life on life's terms. Guide me to hand over the results and not take it personally and to focus on the work at hand...to free myself from those stubbornly held resentments and to make things right. Let me mean what I say, and do what I say, to follow up on the living amends that I make. Give me the wisdom to accept the things I cannot change. Amaze me God.

In Jesus's name,

Amen

* * *

Dear God,

We lean into the third step as we work through the task of placing my heart and mind onto the table to make our amends. We turn our will and our lives over to You, God. Let this reassure us that things will turn out the way they are meant to be. Let us be thorough in this process. Hold our hands, Jesus–let us be guided by Your Everlasting Love. Grace us with the awareness of feeling your love for us. That the results are in Your Hands and all we need to do is let go of control. Let our intentions be pure, to make right what we have wronged. Help us to take accountability for our lives. Grow us up. Guide us to find the right words and to delay–to keep going. Grant me spiritual experiences as I do my amends and I trust the process of how others will respond and to accept and invite You into the fire if the results are not what we want. Let us accept and respect those who we have harmed. For we have grown ever expansive faith in living life on life's terms. Guide us to hand over the results and not take it personally and to focus on the work at hand...to free ourselves from those stubbornly held resentments and to make things right. Let us mean what we say, and do what we say, to follow up on the living amends that we make. Give us the wisdom to accept the things we cannot change. Amaze us God.

In Jesus's name,

Amen

Chapter 10:

Keeping Our Side of the Street Clean (Step 10)

But I say to you who hear, love your enemies,
do good to those who hate you.
-Luke 6:27-28 (NASB)

Things come up: Fear, resentment, frustration. Stuff happens. We get irritated, discontent, ticked off. It just seems to be a part of life, part of the human experience. It's what can pop up when you're living life on life's terms. Instead of avoiding or numbing these things as they appear in our lives, we face them. We can face them head on by doing a daily tenth step.

The AA Big Book instructs us to "continue to watch for selfishness, dishonesty, resentment and fear. When these crop up, we ask God at once to remove them. We discuss them with someone immediately and make amends quickly if we have harmed anyone. Then we resolutely turn our thoughts to someone we can help. Love and tolerance of others is our code."

At first, it seemed like a huge pain to do a Step 10 nightly or even as spot checks throughout the day. When I got to Step 10, my sponsor sent me some tenth step inventory questions that she wanted me to work with. I took one glance and it seemed like a million questions were on it. I balked at first, then avoided it like the plague. I wasn't willing to do what it takes. I didn't pick up the sheet again for months. I point blank refused to do it. I knew at this point in my 12-step journey that faith without works is dead. I had a lot of faith in God and the 12-step program and I needed to just keep going, keep taking action. I was rebelling against doing the work. I knew that I needed to keep my side of the street clean and that it was not only necessary but vitally important for my own sanity and recovery. So I started doing tenth steps.

Was all the effort worth it? Oh, yes! To be cleansed on a daily basis of fear and resentment was a priceless gift. I wrote and then confessed to my sponsor or fellow, and to God, the exact nature of my wrongs, on a day-to-day basis. Miracles began to take root and become a daily occurrence. I had neutrality if I worked this important step. I had freedom if I kept myself "in fit spiritual condition" and not rest on my laurels. I was deep into my recovery now and it felt like with the help of God and others in the program, I could handle anything that came my way, without picking up.

The Discipline of Spiritual House Cleaning Prayer

Dear Heavenly Father,

Show me how to do a daily spot check inventory just for today. Make it second nature to take responsibility for what I say and do throughout the day; to recognize my character defects and to make amends after You reveal my wrongdoings. Also, remind me of my character assets and the good things that happened today. Help me stay willing and patient with myself when I answer the questions to clarify and to clean my side of the street. Give me protection and safety, guidance and courage. Grant me honesty with myself and with others as I hold myself accountable for all that I've done.

Jesus, shine Your Light on the ways that I can expand your kingdom through kindness, inspiration, generosity, love, compassion, forgiveness, responsibility and service work. Find me ways to be of service to others. Grow this practice. Show me the way with Your Everlasting Grace. Give me plenty of opportunities to share my experience, strength and hope in everything that I do. Acknowledge the simple smiles to strangers, helping neighbors, expressing how much I love my friends and family and passing the torch of hope to others who suffer or who long for inspiration. Let me freely give what has been freely given to me. Father God, thank you for forgiving my sins and for renewing my spirit in Your Presence.

Keep me emotionally sober through the important work of the tenth step. Lift me up from being upset, angry or off-balanced. Let me accept what I find when I look inside my conduct for today. Lift me out of fear. Give me the strength to tell my story and to put it on paper, to share it with a fellow. To get clear on it. To learn from it. Iron out those things that are crooked.

Grant me the willingness to be willing to do spot-checks. Quiet my stormy emotions. Grant me serenity after any calamity. Show me how to forgive others, to address all resentments that come up and give me the willingness to pray and forgive those who wronged me. Help me to see my part in it. Convert the painfulness of defects into great assets to bring love into this world, to respect others, to resolve all resentments and keep my ego in check.

Thank You for granting me precious sobriety and for showing me how to clean my house and not rest on my laurels. Saturate me with deep integrity. Let me always stay true to You, God. Show me how to be the best person I can be.

In Jesus's name,

Amen

* * *

Dear Heavenly Father,

Show us how to do a daily spot check inventory just for today. Make it second nature to take responsibility for what we say and do throughout the day; to recognize our character defects and to make amends after You reveal our wrongdoings. Also, remind us of our character assets and the good things that happened today. Help us stay willing and patient with ourselves when we answer the questions to clarify and to clean our side of the street. Give us protection and safety, guidance and courage. Grant us honesty with ourselves and with others as we hold ourselves accountable for all that we have done.

Jesus, shine Your Light on the ways that we can expand your kingdom through kindness, inspiration, generosity, love, compassion, forgiveness, responsibility and service work. Find us ways to be of service to others. Grow this practice. Show us the way with Your Everlasting Grace. Give us plenty of opportunities to share our experience, strength and hope in everything that we do. Acknowledge the simple smiles to strangers, helping neighbors, expressing how much we love our friends and family and passing the torch of hope to others who suffer or who long for inspiration. Let us freely give what has been freely given to us. Father God, thank You for forgiving our sins and for renewing our spirit in Your Presence.

Keep us emotionally sober through the important work of the tenth step. Lift us up from being upset, angry or off-balanced. Let us accept what we find when we look inside our conduct for today. Lift us out of fear. Give us the strength to tell our story and to put it on paper, to share it with a fellow. To get clear on it. To learn from it. Iron out those things that are crooked.

Grant us the willingness to be willing to do spot-checks. Quiet our stormy emotions. Grant us serenity after any calamity. Show us how to forgive others, to address all resentments that come up and give us the willingness to pray and forgive those who wronged us. Help us to see our part in it. Convert the painfulness of defects into great assets to bring love into this world, to respect others, to resolve all resentments and keep our egos in check.

Thank You for granting us precious sobriety and for showing us how to clean our house and not rest on our laurels. Saturate us with deep integrity. Let us always stay true to You, God. Show us how to be the best people we can be.

In Jesus's name,

Amen

Doing a tenth step is like bathing daily. You get to wash away any funkiness of the day by cleaning up at night or even throughout the day to keep yourself clean emotionally, mentally and spiritually. It is about keeping your side of the street clean. People throw their trash outside their car windows and it accumulates and the street gets gritty, dirty and cluttered. Our minds can do the same thing, and a tenth step can clear it all away. It gives us perspective: we have a willingness to look at ourselves and reflect and learn. It can put us back on track after a rough day.

I utilized doing a tenth step in a couple of different ways—spot checks and nightly checks. I admit that I don't do it every SINGLE day. After all, it is progress not perfection.

Spot Checks

Spot checks are done at the time of any disturbance. Someone makes you mad or you feel offended? Time to do a spot check. Did you get some bad news? Time to do a spot check. You work with yourself and include the trinity of God, you and your sponsor—or some other supportive program person—and take responsibility for your part and for those you are angry or disappointed with.

What I learned with spot checks is that you take an upsetting situation and where you're at, through all of the 12 steps. With spot checks I usually answer the questions to myself and to a fellow or my sponsor if I can get a hold of them. Sometimes I'll put pen to paper with a spot check. I will reach out and share and bounce ideas off a trusted fellow to explain the situation, where I'm at and ask for feedback. I will identify the character defects at play and pray to God, asking that they be removed. I will give an apology or amend if the situation calls for one. Tenth steps are like mini-fourth steps. They are inventories. So you can think of them in terms of the columns—who upset you, getting clear on what happened, how it affected you and what your part in it was.

A clear way of doing a spot check is to pull a situation through all of the 12 steps. These are the questions that I'll ask and answer.

- Step 1: What do I have control over and what am I powerless over? (think of the serenity prayer).
- Step 2: Do I believe that God can restore me to sanity? I can't do this alone.
- Step 3: Am I willing to hand the situation over to God, along with my self-will?
- Step 4: With whom do I hold a grievance toward? What happened? How did it affect me and what's my part in it?
- Step 5: Share this situation with a fellow in God's presence.
- Step 6: What character defects are at play?
- Step 7 and 11: Pray to God to remove these defects of character.
- Step 8 and 9: Anyone I owe an amend or even an apology to?
- Step 10: record all of this process or share with a trusted fellow.
- Step 11: Can I spend 5 minutes in prayer and meditation, being quiet with God and praying for all those involved?
- Step 12: Who can I be of service to? Can I help someone else?

Nightly Inventories

BE ANGRY AND yet DO NOT SIN; do not let the sun go
down on your anger,
Ephesians 4:26-27 (NASB)

If you do, you create a lot of toxic thinking, stress, turmoil and obsessive negative thoughts. It causes us to wake up on the "wrong side of the bed" with resentments festering and blood boiling with yesterday's anger and problems. As addicts, rage and resentment are extremely toxic to our recovery. They can create rabbit holes to fall back into our addiction. We are not given the "luxuries" of resentment and unresolved anger, as normal people are, because we can go back into our disease if negativity is burning in our hearts.

The inventory is also a place to acknowledge what good we witnessed and were a part of in our day. How did we help others? What good did someone do for you? What inspiring or wonderful things did we see happen in our day? It's not all about focusing on the negative but taking the whole day into consideration, good, bad and shades of gray.

It's time to put pen to paper and then discuss or send to your sponsor or another trusted program friend. I have gotten into the routine of answering the questions then emailing them to my sponsor as a gesture of surrender.

Creating Your Own Tenth Step Nightly Inventory Sheet

Below are some questions you can ask yourself as part of your nightly inventory. Piece together the questions that resonate with you the most that will both challenge you and provide you with powerful information about yourself. Type these questions into one document–preferably something you can cut and paste into an email if you decide to send to your sponsor. This will also enable you to copy and paste into your journal or a tenth step inventory file you save on your computer. Or if you prefer handwriting your answers, construct a sheet with space to write the answers and make copies for yourself to fill out at night. Mix and match and be sure to include some of the asset questions too, in order to keep things balanced. Add some questions of your own too. Make it your own!

NOTE: If typing the questions, work to get them all on one page. If handwriting, keep them to two or three depending on how much space you want to allot yourself to write in the answers.

Sample questions:
- How was I selfish today?
- How was I resentful today?
- Do a mini fourth step: Who made you mad or got on your nerves? How did it affect you? What part did you play?
- Am I willing to embrace acceptance for those I cannot change?
- Was I dishonest? If so, what was it about?
- Am I willing to get honest with myself and my sponsor and/or trusted fellow in the program?
- Fearful? What were you afraid of?
- Today was I afraid (of losing what I have, not getting what I want, of being found out)?
- Am I willing to turn over my fears and have faith in God instead?
- Did I experience self-pity? What was it about?
- Am I willing to Let Go and Let God?
- Describe moods throughout the day?
- What was the high and low of today?
- How was I self-centered, only thinking about myself?

GRATITUDE:
- What was I grateful for?
- What challenge(s) cropped up that I was grateful for today?
- What have I learned from living this day in my shoes?

GROWTH:
- What was I proud of myself for?
- What showed a good quality of myself?

- What good did I experience or witness?
- What did I do for others ?
- What skills/gifts/talents did I utilize?
- Any AHA moments?
- How did I express my creativity?
- Was I able to get outside myself in a healthy way? When and how?

ASSETS:
- What character asset(s) came into play today?
- Was I willing to inconvenience myself to help another person?
- Did I help another person without being asked?
- How have I been courageous, persevering or determined?
- How have I been humble, grateful or selfless?
- How have I been tolerant, accepting and patient?
- How have I been understanding?
- In what ways was I wise and intuitive?
- Where am I in this present moment? Can I identify, honestly, my true emotions and current mental state?
- What is it that I want? What are my motivations?
- Are my motivations in alignment with my spiritual values and principles?

GLITCHES:
- What did not go right today? List.
- What did the glitch help me to appreciate?

GOALS:
- What are my goals for tomorrow?
- What are some SMART (Specific, Measurable, Achievable, Relevant and Time-bound) baby-step goals I am going to accomplish?
- Where am I heading in terms of achieving my goals?
- How do I need to take care of myself?
- What kind of self-care am I planning for tomorrow?

- Was I inconsiderate?
- Was I kind and loving toward all?
- Do I owe an apology?
- What did I do for others today?
- What did others do for me?
- Have I kept something to myself which should be discussed at once? If so, what?
- What could I have done better?
- What did I do well?
- After seeking God's help, did I then turn my thoughts to someone I could help? What did I do or how can I be of service to others?
- Was I resentful? Describe:
- Was I selfish, self-seeking, dishonest, afraid, prideful, jealous, envious or lazy?
- Did I harm another person?
- Am I willing to forgive the person toward whom I am feeling resentful?
- Am I willing, with prayer, to forgive the person I feel resentment toward?
- Do I owe an amend? If so, am I willing to make one?
- What defect of characters came up today?
- Am I willing to have God remove the defects of character?
- What assets can I strive for tomorrow that will put me more in alignment with God's Will (i.e. humility, trust, intimacy, honesty, contentment, generosity, love, zeal, forgiveness, unselfishness, patience etc.).

Take your situation through the 12 steps

It is important to pray for those who have "wronged" you. It releases toxins from your thoughts and humanizes those you hold resentments toward. This concept is summed up in a story at the back of the AA Big Book called Freedom from Bondage:

"If you have a resentment you want to be free of, if you will pray for the person or the thing that you resent, you will be free...Do it every day for two weeks and you will find you have come to mean it and to want it for them, and you will realize that where you used to feel bitterness and resentment and hatred, you now feel compassionate understanding and love."

When I was working with a sponsor named Donald A., he gave me a copy of a handwritten sheet with questions he had transcribed from his old-timer AA sponsor. Essentially, it was taking your day through the 12 steps and tools in a slightly different way:

- Anything unmanageable in your life currently?
- Any signs of insanity in your thoughts or actions?
- Where is the third step in your problem solving?
- Update 4 & 5: Current fears? Anxiety? Resentments? Shame? Emerging assets?
- Have your defects remained the same? Are some diminishing? Do we need to say the seventh step prayer?
- Do you owe amends? What's your plan to make the amend?
- Let's talk about your prayer life? a.m. p.m.
- What AA literature are you reading?
- What service are you providing at meetings? Making coffee? Set up? Secretary or treasurer?
- Are you greeting newcomers? Making certain they are invited to after-meeting lunches, etc.?

Doing a step 10 always brings me closer to God. I address situations that disturb me as obstacles that are in the way of having a clear connection to Him. I can easily get into self-righteous anger, selfishness and self-centeredness, which take me away from God and into self-will. It is easy to begin to get the mind spinning with thoughts of 'me, me, me' and wanting things my way and trying to control things out of fear. Or playing the victim/martyr role. When I bring God and others in the program into my life by doing a tenth step, I get out of my head, and back into the stream of life where I can help others and contribute to the world.

Chapter 11:

Conscious Contact with God (Step 11)

┌───┐

Step 11: Sought through prayer and meditation to improve our conscious contact with God as we understood Him, praying only for knowledge of His will for us and the power to carry that out.

└───┘

Be anxious for nothing, but in everything by prayer and supplication with thanksgiving let your requests be known to God.
Philippians 4:6 (NASB)

But you, when you pray, go into your inner room, close your door and pray to your Father who sees what is done in secret will reward you.
Matthew 6:6 (NASB)

I wanted to flow with the stream of life that God unfolds throughout each and every moment. To trust in life on life's terms. To trust Him fully, even when I cannot see His Bigger Picture.

I knew that trust happens over time and that if I were to gain trust in God, I had to get to know Him better. I had to have a personal relationship with Him.

The entire 12-step program is chock full of spiritual connection and experiences, aimed at getting to know and leaning into God as the solution. We are powerless over alcohol and only with the help of God could we be restored to sanity and remain sober. In working with Step 11, I really focused on listening and talking to Him in the form of meditation and prayer. It focuses on these two things with the intention to surrender personal will to do His Will.

The Magnificence of Meditation

Experiment with different kinds of mediation because what works for one person, may not work for the next. Remain open-minded. If you are finding that nothing resonates for you, keep working at it! Don't give up. Your relationship with God is too important.

My meditation journey brought me from guided meditations to focusing on an object and then also focusing on me observing that object, to my favorite form: mindfulness meditation as taught by Jon Kabat-Zinn, developer of MBSR (Mindfulness Based Stress Reduction). Mindfulness meditation is a beautiful thing—it really catapulted me into acceptance of the way things are and got me super present. In his book *Mindfulness for Beginners*, Kabat-Zinn defines mindfulness as "awareness, cultivated by paying attention in a sustained way: on purpose, in the present moment, and non-judgmentally."

Mindfulness meditation involves paying attention and anchoring myself to the present by focusing on my breath. I find a quiet, still and serene place to practice. Then I set an alarm for the designated amount of time I want to meditate for. This is a very important step because then I'm not preoccupied with checking how much time has gone by, looking at the clock anxiously for the time to be over. I can just "set it and forget it" and surrender to each precious moment, being totally present, moment by moment to my breath and my wandering mind.

After setting the alarm, I breathe naturally and focus on the sensations of my breath. Where do I feel my breath? Under my nostrils? Do I notice it more strongly in my abdomen rising and falling? Whichever is more prevalent, pay attention to that.

Of course, as a human being, I get distracted and have monkey-mind thoughts come up. Sometimes it can feel like I'm crawling out of my skin if I'm upset over something. My energy is fast. Meditation slows me down. Easy does it. There is no judgment, only an environment of acceptance and compassion. Instead of trying to smash my thoughts or stop them, I let them simply be and when I notice that my attention has shifted to my thoughts, I identify that last thought that I can remember, then consciously and gently bring my attention back to my breath and its sensation in my body (nostril or abdomen).

When I get quiet in this way, often a quiet voice will come to me with some guidance or a word or memory or reminder, an impression, or an image. It's potentially a sign from God. Sometimes it doesn't happen at all, but the more I train my mind to get still and settle in, these divine inspirations come to me.

I always set an intention to rest in the space with God, where inspiration is bound to happen, even if I don't actually hear His voice. Something will come to you at the right time on God's watch. It may not be immediate. It has been helpful for me to rely on some words from the AA Big Book to set an intention before we begin our meditation, "...we ask God for inspiration, an intuitive thought or a decision."

Mediation doesn't have to take much time. It's nice when I can rest into a 30- or 45-minute period, however, it didn't start like that for me. For a long time, 45 minutes seemed like forever. Sometimes my wild monkey mind will spin so fast that I can hardly sit still. If I'm really squirrely, I will set an alarm for just 1-3 minutes. I will sit there, get quiet and breathe, watching my mind drift quickly from thought to thought. For the longest time, I would meditate for 3 or 5 minutes. It's like building muscle. The more you do it, the more you CAN do it, and for longer periods of time. It's a practice. From my experience, it really does make a difference in getting me closer to my Creator.

Another benefit that I noticed is that meditation creates a space, like a couple extra seconds, between incoming stimuli and how I choose to respond to it. There is not as much reaction based on my emotional mind. Rather, it is getting into a sort of wise mind, a more thoughtful, intuitive and calm mind and making decisions from that place instead.

Being Present With Yourself and With God

In 2016, I meditated every day of the year (minus 5 days). I played a game with myself. I got a calendar and drew a big red X with a sharpie for every day that I meditated. I also began a meditation journal, to document my experience. Here are some of my experiences in the early days of meditating on a daily basis:

"I sat down to practice meditation tonight. I am in the midst of establishing a regular formal practice. That means: same place, same time, same bat channel, same chair, day after day. Tonight I didn't want to break away from checking my social media and having a great conversation with a friend, but I did it. I'm so proud of myself."

"My mind wanders and I lose track of my breathing; Jon (Kabat-Zinn) points out that the breath will actually disappear outside of awareness when my thoughts intrude."

"When I first tried this mindfulness meditation, I could not even identify what I was thinking about. I thought there was something wrong with my memory, but the more I practiced, the more I realized that my thoughts were moving so fast that my memory could not keep up with it. I noticed it took a conscious effort to stop and note what the thoughts are about. I used to skip this important step because it was frustrating. I would notice that my mind wandered and just immediately bring my attention back to my breath.

"Identifying my thoughts is an important step. It means cultivating, actively, being present with my thought-life. It is an act of love and care to give myself space to be in touch with my thoughts, even if they are wandering into the mind frequently or being like a monkey or squirrel. It is honoring my mind. Not judging myself. Letting the thoughts kind of float in the air in front of me. Not smashing them or pushing them down. It is a process of befriending my mind, and this leads to total acceptance."

"Today I meditated with the companion of worry. My lower back started hurting about a week and a half ago. There was the companion of pain, panic and worry. I followed the instructions of attending to my breath. My mind wandered to catastrophizing about the state of my back. My heart started beating faster and hurting from all the fear. I acknowledged my thoughts and these strong feelings, and brought myself back to my breath. It was hard at times because the feelings of worry and panic were so strong. It was like reaching into deep waters while keeping my head afloat to catch a sinking anchor. The sinking anchor was my breath. The anchor kept me from being swept up in the storm. Meditating tonight was not pleasant or relieving. There was, however, a small sense that everything will be okay."

"The subtleties of meditation. The breath is so close to your skin and you just need to follow it. Just following your own breath. It makes you pay attention to all other sorts of things outside of meditation. When you are getting upset. When you are feeling gratitude. When it is time to drink some water. It makes these things which are part of life—pop into more awareness."

"Meditation makes me bear witness to my thoughts at any time and bear witness to my emotional state without letting it harm me, even in the midst of feeling overwhelmed. It's not the easiest thing to explain. It's like there is this light that is shining onto every thought and it's a candle that can never be extinguished for as long as I live, and that is my breath. It's like the witness is protection against harming myself with my own thoughts and emotions. I can witness it and feel it without getting tangled in it or acting on it."

You can feel things strongly and not get attached to them. You are able to freely let go of things more easily, even in the midst of a crisis. It feels really good to have this empowerment. It's like you are learning about who you are and what your power is and how to regulate your emotions without running from them or hiding or fighting. You regulate them by paying attention to what is on your mind and by attending to your breath. It is really that simple.

When I am still and quiet and focusing on my breathing, which is a gift from God, I feel closer to my Creator. I get intuitive thoughts and inspirations. God is pleased that I am taking the time to be with Him. He wants me to deepen and expand our relationship. Active listening is a true artform. Not only listening to my own thoughts which sometimes swirl in my head, but to hear or feel "that still soft voice of God."

Meditation is so important in this busy and loud world—to get quiet with yourself and your Creator. It's a time of reflection and listening. Just giving yourself quiet space is a gift. It's being with God. There is nothing better than being with God. You will really deprive yourself of this closeness if you don't give meditation a chance. Even squirrelly minds can learn how to quiet themselves! I'm living proof of that.

<hr>

Conscious Contact With God Prayer

God,

Guide me to embody and act on Your Will. I humbly stand in Your Power. Help me pay attention to Your Symbolism, Your Whispers, Your Inspiration—Your Holy Spirit working through others in the program. Teach me how to actively listen and take action on Your Guidance.

I praise You, Lord. You work in remarkable ways. I can trust You with all my problems—with the burdens of addiction, cravings, sadness and fear. I can leave self-centeredness, pity, selfishness and dishonesty at Your doorstep and trust that You will remove them. Until then, I can act as if You already have.

God, You move mountains. You transform fear into faith. Show me patience for You to work Your Miracles. Give me the willingness to develop the discipline to meditate and pray so I am more receptive and so that I can become closer. Show me that every effort I make along the way strengthens our connection.

Come into the fire with me during trying times. Lift me up out of valleys and teach me what I need to learn. Together let's lay down the foundation of a solid sacred relationship. Help me build the sturdy structures of a friendship with You, Jesus. Grant me discipline to use prayer and mediation to keep in conscious contact with You. Peace and love are Your gifts. I receive them now.

I praise You for all the prosperity, abundance, joy, love, happiness and money You have blessed me with in the past, present and into the future. Through our partnership, dear Lord, let my words and experience touch many lives, to spark hope in the hearts of other addicts. Help me to fulfill my purpose in order to expand Your Kingdom.

Thy Will not mine, be done.

In Jesus's Mighty Name.

Amen

* * *

God,

Guide us to embody and act on Your Will. We humbly stand in Your Power. Help us pay attention to Your Symbolism, Your Whispers, Your Inspiration—Your Holy Spirit working through others in the program. Teach us how to actively listen and take action on Your Guidance.

We praise You, Lord. You work in remarkable ways. We can trust You with all our problems, with the burdens of addiction, cravings, sadness and fear. We can leave self-centeredness, pity, selfishness and dishonesty at Your doorstep and trust that You will remove them. Until then, we can act as if You already have.

God, You move mountains. You transform fear into faith. Show us patience for You to work Your Miracles. Give us the willingness to develop the discipline to meditate and pray so we are more receptive and so that we can become closer. Show us that every effort we make along the way strengthens our connection.

Come into the fire with us during trying times. Lift us up out of valleys and teach us what we need to learn. Together let's lay down the foundation of a solid sacred relationship. Help us build the sturdy structures of a friendship with You, Jesus. Grant us discipline to use prayer and mediation to keep in conscious contact with You. Peace and love are Your gifts. We receive them now.

We praise You for all the prosperity, abundance, joy, love, happiness and money You have blessed us with in the past, present and into the future. Through our partnership, dear Lord, let our words and experience touch many lives, to spark hope in the hearts of others. Help us to fulfill our purpose in order to expand Your Kingdom.

Thy Will not ours, be done.

In Jesus's Mighty Name.

Amen

The Power of Prayer

Access to our Lord, Jesus Christ, is 24/7. He is always there, waiting patiently for us to open the door and let Him in.

Loneliness is the trademark of addiction. I honestly thought that I was the only person experiencing this form of misery from sex and cocaine addiction and from the trenches of an eating disorder: food addiction. The truth is I was never alone. God was holding me in the precious and sacred palm of His Hand. Always there. Gracing me with His Glory. Waiting for me to open the door and let Him.

The 12 steps were the gateway and invitation to get closer to God. Surrendering everything, my will and my life that includes everything-every worry, every victory, every form of sadness, conflict, fear. The program taught me to hand over everything to Him, to my savior Jesus Christ.

For addicts to live a sober life in recovery is indeed a miracle. Without the help of God, it is not possible. We need His help. We need to sacrifice self-reliance and become God reliant if we are to give ourselves any chance of recovery from the devastating pit of despair, the prison of active addiction.

I used to be bashful to talk out loud to God. I felt silly, stupid and goofy. I didn't feel worthy of this inherent connection. The truth is that God loves to hear from you. He likes to hear your prayers. It took some patience in working through my obstacles. It felt awkward at first to begin talking to God, especially out loud. What if he were too busy for me? What if what I said didn't matter? These were all my distorted and negative, low self-esteem thoughts that I projected onto God. I'm happy to say that these character defects were lifted by Him in Step 7.

As with meditation, I started small. I'd say the simple prayer "God help me" or "God give me a burning bush moment." I started making lists of things I wanted clarity on, of things I wanted in my life, of prayers for people I loved, of people I crossed paths with who requested prayer. I slowly started bringing these things into my prayer life.

God wants what's best for me. He knows everything. He can be everywhere all at once. God has a plan for my life. God wants to hear my prayers out loud. He wants me not only to speak His Word but to ask him for what I want. Our words are powerful.

Fast forward a couple decades into today, I pray out loud, morning and night. Some of my prayers are for myself, if others will be helped. I don't see it as being selfish to pray for more money if you plan to take better care of yourself to enable you to better do God's Will. I don't think that it's unreasonable to pray for boatloads of money, if you're planning to feel financial security and help others with the extra, to perhaps pay for someone's rent, become a philanthropist and support programs that bring light and love into the world. God is a generous God. I've been taught by my Pastor Joel Osteen to PRAY BIG!

I pray for others. Anytime someone says to me, "please say a prayer for me" I make sure that I do, either with them, right away or in my own space. I also pray for people who "did me wrong" or who are real challenges in my life. I pray for them everything I want for myself. Doing this humanizes them. My prayers develop and grow my empathy and compassion. It softens resentment and "justified" anger so that I can see them as human beings, instead of mere annoyances.

Now, I have the discipline to consciously be in contact with God. Not just in the morning and at night, but I carve space to connect with Him throughout the day. I will go to the bathroom at work and say the Serenity Prayer. I will take a little break from a social event, step out and say the third step prayer. I will seek ways, moments to connect and talk or pray to God because it is the most important relationship in my life. I will get in my car and before I start it up, I will set my alarm for 3 min and meditate. I will pray on a park bench.

Again, start small. Set an alarm on your phone for a couple different times throughout the day. When it goes off, step out of the room when you can, or go outside and say a short prayer out loud, or one of the 12-step prayers or Serenity Prayer. You can also time your prayer durations such as setting your alarm for 3-minutes and praying until the time is up, until you finish that last thought. Notice how prayer makes you much more connected inside to yourself and with Your Creator.

Two-Way Prayer

A couple of years ago, my sponsor, Elizabeth G., taught me a valuable tool called two-way prayer.

The practice of two-way prayer was based on instruction and insight from a pamphlet written in the 1930s by Chaplain John Batterson, a member of the Oxford Group. The Oxford Group was an Evangelical Christian group that believed in surrendering everything over to God's Will. Bill Wilson, the co-founder of Alcoholics Anonymous, attended the

Oxford Group meetings before he helped form Alcoholics Anonymous and used some of the concepts to develop the 12 steps.

You can locate it by doing some research online. Another place to find it is in the back of the book by Wally Paton called *How to Listen to God-Overcoming Addiction Through Practice of Two-way Prayer*.

First, I would read the rich and wise pamphlet—from beginning to end. This took about 5-10 minutes. I would, if possible, read it out loud so I can hear its powerful words and focus to get in touch with God in this special way.

From the pamphlet and from my sponsor, I was then instructed to get into a meditative state by carving some time to relax, tune in, listen and write by allowing my mind to "go loose."

First, I wrote a simple question at the top of my page to God such as "How should I handle this problem?" or "What is Your Will for me right now?" At times I was more specific if I wanted clarity on an issue I was facing at the time, such as "What should I do about this conflict with Dan?" or "How do I deal with the bullying at work?" or "What are your plans for my book?"

Then, I was told to focus on spending a short period of time writing to record what I heard with this practice of getting in conscious contact with The Lord. I did this by writing down what I heard or felt which included thoughts, impressions, images–the whole nine yards. I recorded whatever passed through my mind and heart.

After this, I was instructed to "test" what I had written in order to check if it was coming from God or just from my self-will thoughts, harsh self-criticism or judgments. After all, you are recording all your thoughts, so most likely your writing will include some self-will.

The pamphlet instructs you to ask yourself if what you've written is "honest, pure, unselfish and loving." God has all of these qualities. Also, ask yourself these questions from the pamphlet—"Is what you've written in line with your duties to your family—to your community? Are these thoughts in line with your understanding of the teaching found in our spiritual literature?"

That is, is it also in alignment with God's Word, the scripture in the Bible?

If the guidance is coming from God, then take action to obey the message or messages you have received. Take the risk and as you obey God's guidance, the pamphlet says, "Carry out the thoughts that have come. You will only be sure of guidance as you go through with it."

Here are some examples of written two-way prayers:

"QUESTION: What am I supposed to do about this big problem at work– my career and my gifts, talents and purpose? What is the right thing to do?

_____

_____

_____

_____

Dear child, Love–love as much as you can. Do kind gestures and let those people know that you love them–the friends and family. Your supervisor, the team, your organization. Open up your time to do My Will.

Get some help because I did tell you there is a lot of TRAUMA ignited with this whole situation.

The flashbacks are not going to kill you. You can correct the distorted thoughts–the negativity of all the original trauma. There are layers and layers of trauma that have been activated by this experience–even before this. Low self-esteem does nobody good–neither you nor the client, nor the world.

You can have pure and utter freedom communicating in your books. Another reason to work on them. It's called freedom of creative expression, and it is a reward and gift of authoring a book with the type of good intentions you have. You have been given a huge opportunity to improve your work if you choose to accept it. It will grow you as a human being.

Make you a more effective communicator. Don't give up on yourself, my precious daughter."

###

"God, what about today?

_____

_____

_____

_____

Child, Focus on me, focus on me this morning. I see, struggling. Child, be patient with your day. It is not your fault–yesterday's conversation with your boyfriend, you needed to get this out. Child, focus on. I am your loving Higher Power and confidant in your life Child, do not put all eggs in the one basket. Child, turn the man over to me, let him go, Child, wrap him in the Blue Blanket and give it to me. Child, believe in yourself. You do not need this man for your Happiness, Child, today keep it simple. Do therapy, homework, make calls, call your brother, call your girlfriends. Child, you have got this. Read Boundary Book. Child, please give me the crashing thoughts as they do not serve you. Child, please know how much your Heavenly Father loves and adores you and you are not alone. Child, I love you, and am behind you 100% You are enough.

I have cleaned up the grammar and spelling on these. Ultimately, grammar and spelling are not as important as the message. Thoughts can come quick, so be prepared to write fast at times. Sometimes it comes out in fragments to capture and record the true essence of the messages. When you feel the question you have written at the top of the page has been answered, stop writing.

This practice has been a game-changer for me. It has really put me in touch with God, and has contributed to the closeness I feel with my Creator.

Chapter 12:

Service as A Way of Life (Step 12)

For you were called to freedom, brethren; only do not turn your freedom into an opportunity for the flesh, but through love serve one another.
Galatians 5:13

In my disease, I only thought of myself. In all of my relationships, I talked about me and my problems. I blamed others, and always took things personally. I was selfish, self-centered and discontented. Basically, miserable. And I found it impossible to get out of myself. I was controlling, my self-will ran riot; I had to do things my way. It was my way or the highway. Everything that fit outside of my way was wrong, criticized and rejected immediately.

I was an adult, yet I acted like a child; it was as if my emotional state had stop developing from an early age. Actually, from the time I started falling into addictive behavior, before my teens. Stunted emotional development was very real. They say you stop growing emotionally when you start using. If you use for decades, like I did, emotional maturity seems nearly impossible. It's like your emotional development is suspended in time. There is no growth. We emotionally act like children and teenagers even though we are in our 30's, 40's, even in our 60's or 70's.

The 12 steps worked magic on my emotional state. It is a design for living a life of integrity and taking responsibility for my actions. My spiritual life became expansive and I accepted and embraced Jesus' unconditional love and forgiveness. I knew that The Lord loved who I was and that I was forgiven for the crazy stuff I did when I was in the disease. This receptivity of God's gifts gave way to being able to forgive myself and even to growing self-love and self-respect.

Another transformative aspect of working a 12-step program is the love of our fellows—in absolute acceptance in being there for each other with phone calls, fellowship at coffee shops and restaurants. Celebrating the joy of freedom from addiction, one day at a time.

There is a responsibility to pass the message on to others, to give back what was freely given to me. We willingly become beacons of God's light–sharing our experience, strength and hope and being generous in helping others.

It is said in AA's Responsibility Pledge:

"I am responsible, when anyone, anywhere, reaches out for help, I want the hand of AA always to be there, and for that I am responsible."

You can substitute any fellowship for AA and it's still the same: we make that commitment to be there for others. To be of service. There is a lot of responsibility in sharing in meetings; to other members one-on-one; to accept an outreach call from someone who is struggling, rather than disregarding the call. By being a responsible member of a 12-step fellowship, you can be a living example of the glorious effects of working this program.

Being of service, or helping others, both in and out of the rooms, deepened my sense of growing integrity and reliability. That in itself was God's Grace blessing me with a more positive way of living. For me, it took the form of volunteering for nonprofits I was passionate about, writing someone I love a greeting card of gratitude, making coffee at the meetings, being available for outreach calls, chairing meetings, helping a neighbor move, cooking a meal for a lonely landlord.

I was the speaker at meetings too—telling my story of what happened before I discovered the 12 steps, what has happened during my involvement thus far and the transformation that miraculously and continuously takes place inside of me and in every corner of my life.

I started taking on trusted servant positions. I started with stepping up to be Literature Chair, ordering books and sobriety coins within the budget that was discussed at group conscience monthly meetings. I learned the 12 Traditions and saw them come into play during my service work. Just being present is a gift you can give someone, smiling at a stranger or helping your neighbor pull weeds from their garden. Service work kept me connected to others and away from drowning in my own problems; it freed me from the character defects of self-centeredness and selfishness.

Similar to the tenth step inventory spot checks, Elizabeth G. showed me how to take any situation through the 12-steps. She called it "twelfth stepping a problem." For instance, If I was struggling with an upsetting situation at work involving a person I was having challenges with, here is how I might take it through all 12 steps:

- Step 1: Am I powerless over the other person?
- Step 2: Do I believe that God can restore me to sanity?
- Step 3: Am I willing to surrender and place the situation into God's loving hands?
- Step 4: What has happened? How did it affect me? What was my part in it?
- Step 5: Share this with another person and God as your witness.
- Step 6: What character defects is this igniting?

- Step 7: Humbly ask God to remove them.
- Step 8: Who have I harmed?
- Step 9: Do I owe an amend or apology?
- Step 10: Am I willing to do a spot check inventory and nightly inventories while going through this?
- Step 11: Can I commit to getting quiet with God through prayer and meditation and accept and be guided by His suggestions and wisdom? Can I do a two-way prayer?
- Step 12: How can I be of service to another? How can I be useful or help someone? Get out of your head and do it.

Being of Service Prayer

Dear Heavenly Father,

Grant me emotional sobriety today. Teach me to stay focused and centered. You inspire me to help others. Equip me with tools and courage to act in order to grow and be useful. Let me stay completely present for the people I cross paths with. Grow my patience, compassion and willingness to reach out and share my experience, strength and hope. Transform me into your servant, God. Continuously iron out my emotions. Open my eyes to your miracles. Keep me connected to others and plugged into the program. Grant me cheerfulness, spiritual experiences, love and serenity, as I live life on Your Terms, God. Grant me spiritual awakenings, with an increase in courage, strength, tenacity and grace to help others. Help me to build connections and let me contribute to expanding Your Kingdom. Grant me freedom. Let the principles of the program travel and expand outside of these rooms and into the world, like a great river. Show me how to be a person of integrity, a person who takes responsibility for themselves. Let me easily and freely give back what has freely been given to me. Make my recovery solid, one day at a time. Show me forgiveness and willingness to do Your Will. Help me always remember that I cannot run the show—that you are in charge, God. My Savior, Jesus, thank you for healing me from the inside out. Thank you for the great faith that You will use me as one of your agents, your students, your employees—to help You to do Your Great Work throughout all of humanity.

In Jesus' Name.

Amen

* * *

Dear Heavenly Father,

Grant us emotional sobriety today. Teach us to stay focused and centered. You inspire us to help others. Equip us with tools and courage to act in order to grow and be useful. Let us stay completely present for the people we cross paths with. Grow our patience, compassion and willingness to reach out and share our experience, strength and hope. Transform us into your servants, God. Continuously iron out our emotions. Open our eyes to Your Miracles. Keep us connected to others and plugged into the program. Grant us cheerfulness, spiritual experiences, love and serenity, as we live life on Your Terms, God. Grant us spiritual awakenings, with an increase in courage, strength, tenacity and grace to help others. Help us to build connections and let us contribute to expanding Your Kingdom. Grant us freedom. Let the principles of the program travel and expand outside of these rooms and into the world, like a great river. Show us how to be a people of integrity, people who take responsibility for themselves. Let us easily and freely give back what has freely been given to us. Make our recovery solid, one day at a time. Show us forgiveness and willingness to do Your Will. Help us always remember that we cannot run the show—that You are in charge, God. My Savior, Jesus, thank you for healing us from the inside out. Thank you for the great faith

that You will use us as your agents, your students, your employees—
to help You to do Your Great Work throughout all of humanity.

In Jesus' Name.

Amen

Chapter 13:

How to Write your Own Prayers

My heart overflows with a good theme;
I address my verses to the King;
My tongue is the pen of a ready writer.
Psalms 45:1 (NASB)

One special way I move closer to my higher power, whom I call God, is through writing prayers. I will start with a piece of fresh paper and pen and get silent. I will breathe deep a few times and then I will start writing. Writing a prayer is a lot like writing a letter to God. It is friendly, respectful and conversational. I speak to God as if he were a close friend, because He is. I trust Him. I pour out my desires, my hopes and my dreams. I express in writing my concerns, my aspirations, my desire to do God's Will instead of my own. I place a lot of what I have learned by working the 12 steps into my prayers.

After I'm done writing a prayer, I will read it out loud in a silent place. This is me praying that written prayer—hearing it now with my physical voice being heard by God. Saying your prayer out loud is very important. It consecrates it. It brings it into this world. Anoints it with your physical voice. You are talking to God.

It takes some time getting used to being fluid and flowing with the conversations that you have with your Higher Power. Remember that it is progress not perfection. Jesus appreciates your efforts to develop and grow your relationship with Him. We let someone get to know us by talking to them. By telling them who we are and what is going on. It's no different with Almighty God.

There is power behind the written word. With a simple pen and piece of paper, we can record our thoughts, longings, desires, emotions. We can get current and present with God. By writing down our prayers, we have a piece of frozen time in which we connected with God and asked Him for things and praised Him for things he's given us, to express gratitude and to worship Him. We illustrate our faith by believing in the words we have written. We can pray to Him over and over again by reading out loud what is on the page. We can put prayers into the "we" version and pray them with our friends and loved ones or even with a recovery group or as a way to close a 12-step meeting.

We can make prayers general or specific. The more specific we can get, the more personal our prayers are and the more we can zoom into what is really going on with us and ask God for help, the more powerful and personal they become. We can deliberately make them more general to encompass more people if we are writing them for a group of people, or we can leave out catered specifics we have written for those "we" versions of the prayer we capture.

Praying becomes an accountability partnership with my Creator. I ask for God's help and then I take his Guidance as it comes and act on it. This could be an intuitive thought; this could be God working through other people, a conversation, an inspiration. I partner with God to help me do the next right thing. We work a program of action.

I often use a method of writing called Mindfulness Writing. It is a powerful way to get in touch with ourselves and literally pour the words out onto the pages. It can put you in an incredible flow. It can get you present with exactly where you are in real time and gives you the power and tools to express that.

In his book ***Calming your Anxious Mind, How Mindfulness & Compassion Can Free you from Anxiety, Fear & Panic***, Jeffrey Brantley describes mindfulness as "compassionate, openhearted, choiceless awareness. It is cultivated by taking the position of an unbiased, attentive witness to your own experience as it happens in the present moment."

There are seven essential attitudes of mindfulness according to Brantley. They are non-judgment, being patient, having a beginner's mind, trusting yourself, non-striving, accepting, and letting go. When we embrace these attitudes, writing comes more smoothly.

How can we embrace these essential attitudes in our writing? We refrain from judging our own words. We accept what we have written. We look at each thought we are recording through a beginner's mind, as if seeing it for the first time with the awe and curiosity of a child. We have compassion for ourselves and hold ourselves in high regard as we fill up the page with words. We trust that our writing is unfolding as it is meant to be. We don't change or edit anything during the creative flow process of mindfulness writing. We accept all our imperfections and keep going. We use a non-striving attitude by not exerting force over what we are trying to convey, over what we are doing. We just let the words come to us and we simply write them down–it is about flowing, not forcing. We let go of the results, the expectations. We let go of each word after it is written and we move on to writing down the next one. We follow our mind's content as we write the thoughts, feelings and words down.

In mindfulness writing we also let go of self-criticism, perfectionism, correct spelling and grammar. This means you don't always have to write full sentences. You can write fragments.

This will challenge most of us. We want things to be a certain way and we took writing class with rules to follow in the English language. This is your invitation to ignore and disregard all of them! Look at it as a total language adventure. Forget about spelling. Use fragments. It's okay. Even a one word sentence is allowed. Brilliant.

In creative endeavors we often judge or criticize ourselves harshly, wondering if we're doing things "right' or wondering if it will be acceptable by most. With this activity it is you and your Higher Power. There are no judgments, no criticisms. Just acceptance, unconditional love and high regard.

Perfectionism is at the heart of procrastination. So many of us were taught as kiddos to strive for something that doesn't exist: perfectionism. We are all perfectly imperfect. Mindfulness writing is an exercise in embracing your own humanity. You can rebel against strict, restrictive, stressful rules you thought you needed to live by—let go, let God (literally!) and really witness the beauty of language flowing from your mind organically and through your pen or your dancing fingers on the keyboard, as you form the words.

Why should we use mindfulness in writing prayers, or mindfulness writing in general? There are many excellent reasons. It will give you a freedom you may have never experienced. A freedom of expression, of following your muse through the words that come into your mind. Mindfulness writing sharpens our focus on the present moment as we capture more details of what we are paying close attention to. We can give ourselves permission to let go of self-criticism and judgment and embrace acceptance of every word that we write. We can feel what we're feeling without judgment, develop self-compassion and express more of where we are and what we want to talk to God about. We can tune in to the safety of being in the present. We don't have to harp on the past or worry about the future. We can invite and allow worlds to flow from every part of us—mentally, emotionally, physically and spiritually in the present moment.

To do a mindfulness prayer writing session, find a private space to write where you will not be interrupted by others. You can bring something comforting to your space, like a little object such as a cross or a stone and a cozy cup of tea or coffee, a blanket for your legs as you sit, a candle or whatever else you want to make the space special and comforting.

Prepare to try this exercise for the first time in absolute silence. Really listen to your thoughts as you record them or write them down. Later you can experiment with music if you're a big music lover like me and try different volume levels while you write. I tend to write prayers in silence.

Settle into your space. Get comfortable. Close your eyes and take 3-10 deep breaths and count them as you breathe. Continue to breathe normally. Keep your eyes closed. Now, imagine a blank canvas or movie theater screen. For those of us that are older, picture a blank outdoor movie theater screen. Let your thoughts come and go as they will, without trying to kill or squash them. Just let them float around and bring your attention back to the screen. Now, open your eyes, set your alarm for 5-20 minutes, and begin writing without stopping the whole time. Keep the pen moving or your fingers typing. If you cannot think of something to write, just write where you're at or capture a thought.

Here's an example: "God give me the serenity. I cannot think of anything else to say in this moment. Boy it's cold in here and grant me the serenity to feel your love, dear Lord. I'm still cold and the words are not coming easily yet. I want to ask God for peace from the situation at work, to stay above the water and not stoop down to their level. God give me sweet sleep tonight. Thank you God for all of my senses, for the emotions that give me signals or cues as to what I am feeling and pointing in the right direction to head. Thanks for my mind. And I just forgot what I was going to say. Shoot. Oh yeah –Thanks for my mind and all my thought life and the creative landscapes of my mind. Boy it's still so cold in here I'll get a cup of tea once this buzzer goes off…"

You get the idea, right? Just work through those times you don't know what to write. Write anyway, so you stay in a flow. The words will come.

The next step is to read your piece to yourself. Read AS IS. Although you may ultimately edit it, it's always a good exercise to see how your mind works, how it can start or stop in flow and how you get back into flow after your mind wanders.

Word Sculpting

You can now enter edit and rewrite mode. Editing is like sculpting. It's making your writing shine like a diamond, polishing, bringing it into more focus. Scratch out the parts you don't want to include in your prayer. Write the prayer double-spaced on paper or on the computer so you can write in some other ideas that come to you. If you want to correct spelling or incorporate any grammatical correctness, feel free to now, but know that you don't have to follow any rules. This is your writing and your time and space to write a prayer to God. It's sacred time. It's your time with God.

After you're finished editing, read it out loud again. Correct again as needed. Put it in the "we" version also if you want.

Some other attitudes you may want to embrace is to talk to God with deep reverence, intimacy, and vulnerability. You can tell God anything. God wants the best for you. You've been through a lot and now you are on the road to recovery. It takes courage to speak to God and a boldness to express what you want.

Some ideas for making your prayers more powerful would be to include scripture from the Bible and phrases, concepts or passages from 12-step literature. Some examples would be:

- Relieve me of my "self-will run riot;"
- Thank you, God, that you are doing for me what I could not do for myself.
- Guide me to not regret my past nor wish to shut the door on it.
- Teach me how to be rigorously honest with myself and with my sponsor.
- God, heal this spiritual hole in my heart with Your Love.
- You said by Jesus's stripes I am healed. Thank you God, for your healing. God, thank you for the hedge of protection you have around me. Job 1:10 says, "Have you not put a hedge around him and his house and all that he has, on every side? You have blessed the work of his hands, and his possessions have increased in the land."
- Thank you, Lord, for increasing my productivity, my prosperity.
- Thank you that no weapon formed against me shall prosper.
- God, keep my emotions in check as I begin the fact-finding mission of working my fourth step.

- God, show me the difference between what I can and cannot change.

Feel free to use anything above or anything you find in the prayers written in this book, but make them your own.

Use descriptive verbs and words when asking for God's help: ***Grant*** me strength; ***Show*** me your guidance. ***Give*** me a burning bush moment. ***Relieve*** me of the insanity of compulsive thinking. ***Eradicate*** negative thinking. ***Love*** me until I love myself.

If you don't ask ask ask then the answer is an automatic no, points out Jack Canfield, author of *The Success Principles*. Don't underestimate the power of big prayers. Ask big! "Pray bold prayers," says my pastor Joel Osteen. Ignite your prayers with your dreams. Don't hold back! Although it might not be as black and white, cut and dry in God's case, really put yourself out there. Let God know what you want.

Praise God while you're praying, as part of your prayer. God loves to be praised for all the ways He solves our problems, all His miracles. In faith, thank Him for the results He has yet to grant you, as if it has already happened. Express gratitude. Don't take things for granted. Infuse your prayers with gratitude. Our Heavenly Father is the Creator of everything. He likes to hear us praise Him. It is a form of worship.

One prayer that I pray often is, "Thank You God for all the abundance, wealth, money, prosperity and love You've given me in the past, present and into the future." I praise God for what he's done for me, what he is presently doing and thank him for everything he will do for me in the future. It takes faith to pray these kinds of prayers. Praise infused with faith goes well together.

Another way to approach your prayer writing is to incorporate a two-way prayer practice into it. (Read more about this in Chapter 11). Imagining The Holy Spirit working through you with an intention of prayer and praise to Him is really powerful. It's a process but definitely worth it if you carve some time for it.

Some other tips:

- Surrender to the idea that you need help from Almighty God. Express that to Him.
- Speak from your heart.
- Ask for God's help to write a prayer.
- Develop a writing routine by writing at the same time every day and do three morning pages of writing everyday. Get current with yourself and talk to God about your prayers. Write about anything to keep the flow going. As Bob Goff, author of *Undistracted* once advised me, if I feel blocked and don't know what to write about, "Write about all the animals in the zoo."
- Explore: What are you struggling with currently in your life, in your recovery, your job, your relationships, your body, mind, spirit? What about emotionally? What step are you working on? What parts of your recovery program need tightening up?
- Ask your friends to pray with you or read the prayer out loud to someone. It makes it so you are praying together.
- Having faith that your prayers are heard and that those things will show up in your life if it is God's Will, and on His watch.
- Review the chapter on Step 11 for additional insight into prayer and its companion, meditation.
- Prepare for writing your prayer by brainstorming a list of things you want to touch on in your prayer—then put them in the order that makes most sense. Then just follow the outline when you write your prayer.

Writing prayers can really increase your conscious contact with God. It can give you tremendous peace and the knowledge that you are never alone. You can be a blessing to others by praying with them with the prayers you have written.

If you need to speak your prayer out loud to someone and you cannot reach any of your friends, family or fellows, feel free to leave me a message on my voicemail. My number is 720-326-1972.

Chapter 14:

More 12-step Inspired Prayers

You will seek Me and find Me when you search
for Me with all your heart.
Jeremiah 29:13 (NASB)

Here are some more prayers that you can use as inspiration to write your own or to pray by yourself or with others. I also include an introduction to each prayer, which you can experiment with in your own writings.

Sweet Sleep and Gratitude Prayer

Sometimes at the end of the day, my head is swirling and I am exhausted. I've got the "T" in HALT going on big time (HALT stands for Hungry, Angry, Lonely, Tired). Sometimes I feel the satisfaction of helping others and I need my cup refilled with leisure, peaceful activities and fun. At other times, I just need to go to bed early. There are those times where I feel depleted, overwhelmed and triggered.

At times, I'll grab some inspiring reading material, be guided by the grace of God to read or listen to Biblical scripture, or about fear in the AA's big book on page 67, or a story in the back of the book. I'm so happy to have calming material to read. It gives my mind something to focus on.

The more I work the program, the more I experience gratitude for my life and am able to express the gratitude for the gifts that God gives me. The gifts I am now open to receiving. They say the worst day in recovery is better than the best day in the disease. For this, I can count my blessings before I go to bed, and wake up refreshed to a brand new day tomorrow.

～～⚜～～

God,

Cool me down with calmness. Slow down the frantic pace of my fast beating heart and racing mind. Ease me into Your sunset and bless me with beautiful sweet sleep tonight. Wake me up refreshed. Cradle me in Your glorious sunshine once again. Open my ears to hear Your Holy Spirit directing my every step.

Thank you for this sacred replenishment of deep rest upon awakening, let my voice rise up with Your Hope and Inspiration like sapphires at my throat. Anoint me with Your never-ending, everlasting love. Let it pour through me like an ancient peaceful fountain.

Whisper in my ear all your clear instructions. I am Your child and You are my Holy Father. I am listening to You in the silence of the night. Give me peaceful dreams. Let me realize that You are there for me at every crossroads, at the top of every staircase, around every nook and cranny of my life. Bless me with feeling Your Love as I drift off into safe slumber.

You saved and blessed my life with Your Healing Hands. I am Your miracle. I praise You for right-sizing me to walk away from the addiction and to become humble instead. Fill me up with ideas, inspirations and ways to express Your gifts working through my soul, as I rest in Your loving hands. Thank You for granting me tranquility and colorful glory. Give me the awareness of Your Blessing that I am safe in this world. Thank You for Your hedge of protection around my life. You said no weapon formed against me will prosper. Tomorrow help me to think before I speak. Let my words be shaped by Your Power,

Your Grace, Your Love. Discipline me to meditate and pray every day. Lift all strife from my mind as You bless me with precious sleep tonight. I look forward to the joy of the morning.

In Jesus's name I pray,

Amen

* * *

God,

Cool us down with calmness. Slow down the frantic pace of our fast beating hearts and racing minds. Ease us into Your sunset and bless us with beautiful sweet sleep tonight. Wake us up refreshed. Cradle us in Your glorious sunshine once again. Open our ears to hear Your Holy Spirit directing our every step.

Thank You for this sacred replenishment of deep rest. Upon awakening, let our voices rise up with Your Hope and Inspiration like sapphires at our throats. Anoint us with Your never-ending, everlasting love. Let it pour through us like an ancient peaceful fountain.

Whisper in our ear all Your clear instructions. We are Your children and You are our Holy Father. We are listening to You in the silence of the night. Give us peaceful dreams. Let us realize that You are there for us at every crossroads, at the top of every staircase, around every nook and cranny of our lives. Bless us with feeling Your Love as we drift off into safe slumber.

You saved and blessed our lives with Your Healing Hands. We are Your miracles. We praise You for right-sizing us to walk away from the addiction and to become humble instead. Fill us with ideas, inspirations and ways to express Your gifts working through our souls, as we rest in Your loving hands.. Thank You for granting us tranquility and colorful glory. Give us the awareness of Your Blessing that we are safe in this world. Thank You for Your hedge of protection around our lives. You said no weapon formed against us would prosper. Tomorrow help us to think before we speak. Let our words be shaped by Your

Power, Your Grace, Your Love. Discipline us to meditate and pray every day. Lift all strife from our minds as You bless us with precious sleep tonight. We look forward to the joy of the morning.

In Jesus's name I pray,

Amen

Healing Spiraling Shame Prayer

When I was in the disease, I was in a continuous shame spiral. I would lapse then I would be in a state of remorse, self-pity and depression. This became emotionally unbearable. After the bender, I would swear that I would never do it again. I promised myself that this was the last time, that tomorrow I would gather up the strength of my self-will to never do it again. The next day the shame was so unbearable that I was crawling out of my skin and it felt like I had no choice but to numb it. I used again. Things were grim. I struggled with the tremendous weight of depression and when I went out into the world, it felt like people could see right into my life and know that I was not only doing harmful things to myself and others, but that I was a bad person, through and through. My shame would keep me from reaching out to others for help. It kept my sickness a secret. Not a word spoken. Just suffering alone in the pain of the insanity of powerlessness and unmanageability. Just me… abandoning God. Isolation and time on my hands to either think too much, sleep or get high. There was no room to accomplish anything else or to work on myself. The disease of addiction was powerful and all-consuming. When I discovered the 12 steps, I went to as many meetings as I could. I heard my story from the others in the room and that brought me great comfort for the duration of the meeting. The more I worked the steps, spent time with my new program friends and did service work, the more genuine my confidence grew. I was as sick as my secrets and now I had an outlet to share, in real-time, exactly where I was at. I began to do esteem-able things and this in turn erased the unbearable shame that I had known for decades. It was no less than a miracle by the grace of God.

Dear God,

I praise You for leading me to the Program; for the awareness and the awakenings. As I do the work, more of Your Plan for my life will be revealed. Grow my mustard seed faith into the knowledge that the best is yet to come. Evict all lingering negative and persecuting thoughts. Lift the unbearable burden of shame. Dissolve the guilt from the internalized stigma that all addicts are bad people. Heal the shame of lies, deception, manipulation, self-centeredness and selfishness. Remove all my shortcomings. Show me how sick I was and that my actions in the disease were not who I truly am. With Your Wisdom, correct the distortion that if I make a mistake, I am a mistake. Show me Your Mercy and depths of Grace and Forgiveness. Wash me clean of beating myself up for every imperfection, for every mistake, for every memory.

Light up the path of self-forgiveness. Free me from perfectionism. Bring acceptance into my life. Help me to realize that I am your masterpiece, worthy of happiness, serenity and freedom. Teach me how to use my experience to help others extinguish their own sense of shame. Let me soar like an eagle in flight. Create confidence out of confusion; high self-esteem out of heavy shame.

In Christ's name I pray.

Amen

* * *

Dear God,

We praise You for leading us to the Program; for the awareness and the awakenings. As we do the work, more of Your Plan for our lives will be revealed. Grow our mustard seeds of faith into the knowledge that the best is yet to come. Evict all lingering negative and persecuting thoughts. Lift the unbearable burden of shame. Dissolve the guilt from the internalized stigma that all addicts are bad people. Heal the shame of lies, deception, manipulation, self-centeredness and selfishness. Remove all our shortcomings. Show us how sick we were and that our actions in the disease were not who we truly are. With Your Wisdom, correct the distortion that if we made a mistake, we are a mistake. Show us Your Mercy and depths of Grace and Forgiveness. Wash us clean of beating ourselves up for every imperfection, for every mistake, for every memory.

Light up the path of self-forgiveness. Free us from perfectionism. Bring acceptance into our lives. Help us to realize that we are your masterpiece, worthy of happiness, serenity and freedom. Teach us how to use our experience to help others extinguish their own sense of shame. Let us soar like an eagle in flight. Create confidence out of confusion; high self-esteem out of heavy shame.

In Christ's name I pray.

Amen

Anxiety and Depression Prayer

I was experiencing the worst depression of my life when I was spiraling to reach my bottom, I was living the life of a fully dedicated cocaine addict, sex addict and even took it as far as prostituting myself. I lived for a higher high—the more intense and dangerous, the better. The things I used to do didn't give me the hit that I wanted and needed. I wanted so badly to escape so I increased my use of hard drugs to mask the depression. I was laughing and "partying" on the outside, but suicidal and self-destructive on the inside. The drugs were the only thing I lived for. I looked in the mirror and saw myself, my hollowed out eyes and poor complexion and saw the energy drained from my eyes. One time I whispered to myself, "Lisa Jo, you look like death warmed over."

I was heavily medicated for Complex PTSD and Bipolar I. At one point the shrink had me on 16 different medications. What he was doing wasn't working and I made no effort to advocate for myself. I had given up. I was in the worst depressive episode of my life. I was desperate. So instead of taking my own life, like I had tried to before, I made the unconscious decision to kill myself slowly, to obliterate all the emotional pain that was unbearable through the use of substance. I had given up fighting for my life until I came into the 12-step rooms. Literally, the program, with God's Grace, saved my life. Forever I am grateful.

Father God,

Relieve me of depression and anxiety. Boost my stability. I praise You and put my trust in You, God. Spark action to get me out of bed, to take care of myself, along with the courage to ask for help. Grant me trust in Your Timing. Free me from the bondage of self. Counsel me. You said in Proverbs 16:24 (NIV) that "gracious words are a honeycomb, sweet to the soul and healing to the bones." Heal me to the bone. Show me how to extend Your Grace to myself. Put me in touch with purpose and joy. Take away the misery, Teach me self-compassion and acceptance. Show me how to treat myself like Your Masterpiece. Prevent me from kicking myself when I'm down and wrap a blanket of self-forgiveness and compassion around me. Get me out of bed to begin my day. Help me to take a shower, make breakfast and get dressed in clean clothes. Inspire me to call a friend or go to a meeting.

Calm my nerves. Show me what I can do to make the anxiety go down. Come into the fire with me and pull me to safety. Show me to act in accordance with Your Will, God. Guide me to work with a healthy and competent mental health team. Bless my soul with Your

Healing Touch. Take away the toxic shame. Keep me off the substance. Help me find my true self. Thank You for restoring me to sanity. Keep me on the beam with my step work and in using the tools of the program to take action and to stay connected to You and others.

Thy Will (not mine) be done.

Amen

* * *

Father God,

Relieve us of depression and anxiety. Boost our stability. We praise You and put our trust in You, God. Spark action to get us out of bed, to take care of ourselves, along with the courage to ask for help. Grant us trust in Your Timing. Free us from the bondage of self. Counsel us. You said in Proverbs 16:24 (NIV) that "gracious words are a honeycomb, sweet to the soul and healing to the bones." Heal us to the bone. Show us how to extend Your Grace to ourselves. Put us in touch with purpose and joy. Take away the misery, teach us self-compassion and acceptance. Show us how to treat ourselves like Your Masterpiece. Prevent us from kicking ourselves when we're down and wrap a blanket of self-forgiveness and compassion around us. Get us out of bed to begin our day. Help us to take a shower, make breakfast and get dressed in clean clothes. Inspire us to call a friend or go to a meeting.

Calm our nerves. Show us what we can do to make the anxiety go down. Come into the fire with us and pull us to safety. Show us to act in accordance with Your Will, God. Guide us to work with a healthy competent mental health team. Bless our souls with Your Healing Touch. Take away the toxic shame. Keep us off the substance. Help us find our true selves. Thank You for restoring us to sanity. Keep us on the beam with our step work and in using the tools of the program to take action and to stay connected to You and others.

Thy Will (not ours) be done.

Amen

Stay in Today Prayer

Yesterday is gone. Tomorrow may never come. I only have… right now. This precious day. It always felt like too much to commit to something for years, months or days on end. Feels nerve racking and overwhelming. To make a perfect lifetime commitment to sobriety, all at once, seems daunting, even impossible.

Getting there One Day at a Time is more tangible. I could take manageable action steps by staying in today. Throughout my recovery, with the help of a sponsor, I've constructed and committed to simple daily plans in order to stay sober, just for today. These were like baby steps I could take, just for today. I didn't have to commit to tomorrow. Just today. I could take positive action, just for today, For the next 24 hours, I can surrender all cravings. Sometimes things had to be broken down to one hour, one minute at a time, one split second at a time. Going to a meeting was 60 minutes of my day that I was sober. I could sit there listening to people's shares. Then I only had 23 more hours to the day to stay sober.

What was I going to do for the next hour, the next moment? How was I going to stay in the day, in the solution, in recovery? This got me through many trigger days when I was on the verge of going back to the self-destructive behavior of using. By God's Grace and a simple action plan, just for today I could stay sober and continue stringing together days, months and years of recovery time.

Dear God,

Please keep me sober just for today. Today is all You have given me for now. Stop me from harping on the past or projecting into the future. Help me stay present, moment by moment. Stir me to action to do Your Will, one split second at a time. Guide me to do the next best indicated step that You have whispered into my ear and communicated to me through my intuition. Remove all the lies, disappointments and fears from my heart. Help me to make simple plans to get through this day with the precious gift of emotional sobriety. Show me how the past dissolves into a bright new day. Shine Your light through every cell in my body, healing and protecting me in every corner of my mind, body, spirit. Thank You for being with me from sun up to sun down and all through the night. Show me how to focus in this mindful moment. Just for today, wave Your Strong Flag of Unconditional and Everlasting Love into my life, through my awareness, always and forever, one day at a time.

In the name of Christ I pray,

Amen

* * *

Dear God,

Please keep us sober just for today. Today is all You have given us for now. Stop us from harping on the past or projecting into the future. Help us stay present, moment by moment. Stir us to action to do Your Will, one split second at a time. Guide us to do the next best indicated step that You have whispered into our ears and communicated to us through our intuition. Remove all the lies, disappointments and fears from our hearts. Help us to make simple plans to get through this day with the precious gift of emotional sobriety. Show us how the past dissolves into a bright new day. Shine Your light through every cell in our bodies, healing and protecting us in every corner of our minds, bodies, spirit. Thank You for being with us from sun up to sun down and all through the night. Show us how to focus in this mindful moment. Just for today, wave Your Strong Flag of Unconditional and Everlasting Love into our lives, through our awareness, always and forever, one day at a time.

In the name of Christ we pray,

Amen

Tools of The Program Prayer

I picked up many power tools to strengthen my life in recovery: writing, literature, meetings, the telephone, step work, being of service, action plans, anonymity and sponsorship. Each was another layer of protection between me and the use of my drug of choice. I had a plan with agenda items for my day because addiction, like any mental disease, does not like structure. It wants free open reign to mess with your mind. It wants you to be self-absorbed, thinking too much and getting overwhelmed. Getting out of my head and to a meeting or helping someone, is the opposite of my addict's self-centeredness and self-obsessive nature.

God,

Grant me sobriety today. I want to stay focused and centered in You, God. You told me that I can do all things through Christ. Lead me to a happy and fulfilling, purposeful life. Equip me with Your armor and program tools to keep my recovery strong. Anoint me with the courage to act in order to both grow and help others. Expand my patience, my love, my tranquility. Assist me in letting go of all obsessions by getting to a meeting, to share where I'm at and to listen to what other recovering addicts have to say. Show me how to gain more traction away from the addiction by guiding my decisions and helping me play out where actions will take me, like a movie. Make it clear for me to play out the consequences of my actions before I take action. Let me see my sponsorship as a trinity—my sponsor, me and You, Dear Lord. I place this addiction at your feet and pick up the tool of literature. I read from the Big Book and other 12-step literature—to focus and bathe my mind in the truth of recovery. I read scripture from the Bible to inspire and enlighten me with Your Truth. Grow my ambitions to do step work and to work with other addicts in sponsorship, outreach and fellowship. I want to be closer to you, God. Show me how best to be of service to You and my fellows in every given moment. Lift me higher and higher so I can be of maximum service to Your Mighty Kingdom.

In Jesus's Name I pray,

Amen

* * *

God,

Grant us sobriety today. We want to stay focused and centered in You, God. You told us that we can do all things through Christ. Lead us to a happy and fulfilling, purposeful life. Equip us with Your armor and program tools to keep our recovery strong. Anoint us with the courage to act in order to both grow and help others. Expand our patience, our love, our tranquility. Assist us in letting go of all obsessions by getting to a meeting, to share where we are at and to listen to what other recovering addicts have to say. Show us how to gain more traction away from the addiction by guiding our decisions and helping us play out where actions will take us, like a movie. Make it clear for us to play out the consequences of our actions before we take action. Let us see our sponsorship as a trinity—our sponsor, us and You, Dear Lord. We place this addiction at your feet and pick up the tool of literature. We read from the Big Book and other 12-step literature—to focus and bathe our minds in the truth of recovery. We read scripture from the Bible to inspire and enlighten us with Your Truth. Grow our ambitions to do step work and to work with other addicts in sponsorship, outreach and fellowship. We want to be closer to you, God. Show us how best to be of service to You and our fellows in every given moment. Lift us higher and higher so we can be of maximum service to Your Mighty Kingdom.

In Jesus's Name we pray,

Amen

Lead me to Serenity Prayer

Before the program, I rarely experienced serenity. I recall when in Bali, I snorkeled for the first time. Every cell in my body relaxed for the very first time. Fast forward, I entered a 12-step meeting for the first time. When someone spoke and shared parts of their stories and their feelings, I relaxed like that again. These were my people and I was not alone. I thought that I was the only person on the planet to go through the hell that I did when I was using. I had isolated myself, had pushed away all my friends and family. The only people who I associated with had to do with the addiction—other users, manipulators, drug dealers. I've experienced many spiritual awakenings since entering the program. It has brought me tremendous relief from anxiety and has given me such a deep sense of serenity. I am no longer crawling out of my skin. Through working a 12-step program, I feel at home in my body and mind.

Dear God,

I pray for the willingness to be willing to hand over my will and life to You. Guide me through a day of abstinence from addiction, from compulsive and obsessive thoughts and actions. Protect me from triggers. Carry me into a state of surrender to You. Grant me serenity as I place my hand in Yours. Walk me into a calm, serene, accepting existence. Help me to conquer overwhelming situations by focusing on what I can and cannot change and leave the results to You, God. Give me freedom from self will. Let me be of maximum service to You and to others. Pour Your Grace all over me. Saturate me with Your Love. God, I praise You for taking away the stress in my bones. Thank You for blessing me with Your Presence, Lord, and with others in the program. Keep me safe and connected. I praise You Jesus, for all the miracles You perform in my life.

Thy Will (not mine) be done.

In Jesus's name.

Amen

* * *

Dear God,

We pray for the willingness to be willing to hand over our will and lives to You. Guide us through a day of abstinence from addiction, from compulsive and obsessive thoughts and actions. Protect us from triggers. Carry us into a state of surrender to You. Grant us serenity as we place our hands in Yours. Walk us into a calm, serene, accepting existence. Help us to conquer overwhelming situations by focusing on what we can and cannot change and leave the results to You, God. Give us freedom from self will. Let us be of maximum service to You and to others. Pour Your Grace all over us. Saturate us with Your Love. God, we praise You for taking away the stress in our bones. Thank You for blessing us with Your Presence, Lord, and with others in the program. Keep us safe and connected. We praise You Jesus, for all the miracles You perform in our lives.

Thy Will (not ours) be done.

In Jesus's name.

Amen

Faith Without Works is Dead Prayer

The 12-step program is one of action. Merely thinking my way out of things never worked because it was my thinking that got me into this mess to begin with. I had to do something different. In my disease, all I did was chase after my drug of choice to get high. Being an addict robbed me of taking action to better myself in all ways. It consumed me completely. People in the meetings showed me examples of getting more involved in life, to contribute to life by helping others.

In recovery, I could listen to my intuition, God's inspiration, and have faith by taking positive action toward these inspirations. I could trust God and do things to improve my life and leave the self-destruction behind.

Dear God,

Direct my thinking. Bring me into my body to identify what I am feeling in real-time. Give me the courage to take action even when I don't want to. Show me how to surrender everything to You, for You are my Creator and Greatest Ally. Help me to embark on the tenth step spot checks and nightly inventories–to look at myself honestly, to continue taking action on the faith You have placed in my heart. You've said that the best is yet to come. I believe You, Jesus.

Tone down all compulsive and excessive thinking by getting me out of my head and into my body–with exercise and service. Give me happiness, fun experiences, joy and freedom. Show me how to follow Your Direction, even in the face of fear or resistance.

God, You have told me that addiction hates structure. Grant me the energy and time to sit down and write out an action plan for the following day. Keep me on track. Be there, guiding my pen. Show me how to live a balanced healthy life, to structure my time to take good care of myself and to live in active recovery.

Thank You God, for those people in the program who have acted as Your agents to guide me in making action plans and teaching me to do inventories to prevent relapse. Bless all who have given me their experience, strength and hope of how they used program tools and worked the steps. Reveal to me what the next best indicated step is to be. Grant me faith in a better future and let me act upon that faith. I praise You for my tranquility and love, and for Your Closeness.

In Jesus's Mighty Name.

Amen

* * *

Dear God,

Direct our thinking. Bring us into our bodies in identifying what we are feeling in real-time. Give us the courage to take action even when we don't want to. Show us how to surrender everything to You, for You are our Creator and Greatest Ally. Help us to embark on the tenth step spot checks and nightly inventories–to look at ourselves honestly, to continue taking action on the faith You have placed in our hearts. You've said that the best is yet to come. We believe you, Jesus.

Tone down all compulsive and excessive thinking by getting us out of our heads and into our bodies–with exercise and service. Give us happiness, fun experiences, joy and freedom. Show us how to follow Your Direction, even in the face of fear or resistance.

God, You have told us that addiction hates structure. Grant us the energy and time to sit down and write out action plans for the following day. Keep us on track. Be there, guiding our pens. Show us how to live a balanced healthy life, to structure our time to take good care of ourselves and to live in active recovery.

Thank you God, for those people in the program who have acted as Your agents to guide us in making action plans and teaching us to do inventories to prevent relapse. Bless all who have given us their experience, strength and hope of how they used program tools and worked the steps. Reveal to us what the next best indicated step is to be. Grant us faith in a better future and let us act upon that faith. We praise You for our tranquility and love, and for Your Closeness.

In Jesus's Mighty Name.

Amen

Chapter 15:

Food Addiction

'For I know the plans that I have for you,'
declares the Lord, 'plans for welfare and not
for calamity to give you a future and a hope.
Jeremiah 29:11 (NASB)

Hi. My name is Lisa Jo and I'm a compulsive overeater and sugar addict and my life has become unmanageable.

Powerlessness: A Step One Issue

To this day, I am powerless over certain foods. It's similar to how the alcoholic has an allergic reaction toward liquor as mentioned in Alcoholics Anonymous's Big Book in the section called *The Doctor's Opinion*, toward the front of the book. I have an allergic reaction to certain compulsive food behaviors and food items, such as sugary sweets. That means, once I take that first compulsive bite, the phenomenon of craving holds me in its grip and I cannot stop eating, no matter how hard I try.

The more I try to "eat like a normal person," or think that I can, the more I go down the rabbit hole. My definition of eating like a normal person is having one desert after a meal, or having a couple slices of delicious NY-style pizza and stopping there, even if there is a whole cake in my house or an extra large pizza. Or eating an occasional fast food and it being a one time event. Like every 2-3 months. Not a big deal. Not something to obsess over.

It's never like that for me. I've proved this over and over again. They say in the AA Big Book that all addicts' great obsession is to drink like "normal" people and we pursue this to insanity or death. Food addiction is the same way. It's just that the killing happens slower than cocaine or sex addiction.

Addiction recovery is certainly not easy, regardless of the drug of choice. Compulsive overeating or eating disorders of any kind are especially challenging. Why? You have to eat to live. You have to take the tiger out of the cage three times a day. Three meals. At least. Then there are snacks, too; depending on what you've developed as your food plan. We can survive without another drink of alcohol or doing recreational drugs. However, food is the fuel we rely on in order to live.

The trenches of food addiction are tumultuous. Absolute misery. It is ruthless as well as cunning, baffling, all-consuming and powerful. The good news is it is not more powerful than our Mighty Lord, Jesus Christ.

One of the consequences of binge eating for a lot of us, is weight gain. Bigger people in the Western World are considered unappealing, less than, ugly and are shamed by a large majority. People who struggle with their weight are looked down on; considered lazy. I have had the experience of being shunned and looked down upon. Not everyone, of course. There are millions and billions of folks who don't buy into the stigma, and love regardless of weight, can peer into our hearts and love us no matter what. The stigma unfortunately is still there, even with the groundbreaking work of several people, including the creative billionaire singer and entrepreneur, Rihanna. Through her Savage X-Fenty line, she is making beautiful clothes and lingerie for all body shapes and sizes. She puts together fashion shows with models with imperfections or extra weight, to show a person's beauty.

It's tough being a bigger woman in America. Some men avoid eye contact with me just because my body is bigger than what is considered "acceptable" by society's standards. It's like they don't even want to give me a chance. Some people look through me as if I am not there. Some people scoot way over when I'm walking past, acting as if I am twice the size that I actually am. I would say that although this is not the majority of people, it is a hurtful presence nonetheless. There is already enough shame attached to the act of compulsive overeating without anyone else adding to it. We are our own worst critic, and many of us live disgusted by our own out-of-control behavior. Disappointment. Regret. Sadness. Remorse. Even self-hatred. These are the negative messages of the enemy trying to keep us in the bondage of addiction.

My Food Story

As a child, growing up in a war zone, I spent most of my time terrified and on edge. It was always like walking through a minefield--I never knew what to expect from my father's rage. Bombs went off when I least expected. There were cruel words and violent outbursts thrown at me even as a young girl.

I walked on pins and needles throughout my entire childhood, my teens and some of my adult life. I desperately looked for means to escape emotional pain.

Sugar as Heroin

As a little girl, 3 to 4 years old, my brother and I would go to Walgreens with my mom. While she waited for a prescription, or shopped in the rest of the store, my brother and I hung out in the vast, endless candy aisle and proceeded to pick out whatever we wanted. My mother would buy us the candy with little or no restrictions. I remember the candy cigarettes vividly and a wide array of candy bars and Brach candies--the ones that sell by the pound. I would get high off the anticipation of eating all that candy. The visual scene of a bright colored aisle with all that candy started to numb my physical and emotional pain of living in terror of my father. The addictive experience started with the rituals surrounding the addiction. In this case it was shopping at Walgreens or any other place where there was unhealthy food. I would use my imagination of consuming it, the sound of the candy wrappers, getting lost in the colors and smells, watching the items being rung up and put into neat bags. Lining the candy up at home in front of the TV and unwrapping them one by one, taking the delightful contents out for me to sink my teeth into.

When we got home, I would sit and eat, usually in front of the television. The taste and the effect of the sugar took me to another place. A rewarding space, a forgiving place. The food did not shout at me, nor did it hit me. It felt peaceful to let my mother nurture me with food. It made me feel temporarily safe and loved. I was no longer worried about the future and what kind of humiliation or physical abuse was to come. I was also able to climb out of past hurts and get completely present by focusing on the taste—the hypnotic sweetness and then stuffing my feelings way down with the large amounts of sugar at hand. Sugar became my savior. It was my Higher Power.

My mom would feed us sugary sweets as her way of treating us, rewarding us, soothing us. My mom was also a very good cook and she baked. There were always homemade chocolate chip cookies available and a lot of sugary cereals stocked up in the pantry, along with sweets from the snack aisles in the cupboards. I would spend hours looking at all the snack options, grabbing one or two of each one, preparing to binge in front of the television. It became a daily ritual. Actually, several times a day. After I binged, I'd always go back for more. I couldn't get enough sugar. It was like a black hole. And it had a grip on my whole childhood.

On the weekend, there would be boxes of donuts or homemade waffles with tons of syrup. As I consumed these things, I was disassociating from all the emotional pain I carried from growing up in domestic violence. I abused food nearly from the start. I was encouraged to do so by both of my parents. My environment supported the addiction. Sugar was all around me and readily available at all times. If we ran out, my mother would quickly bake some more or stock up the cabinets with sugary sweets.

I vividly remember binging on food during the holidays. This was the prime season for comfort foods. Gorging on sweets. Three or four different pies, and having two slices instead of one with tons of whipped cream. I watched my father be soothed with sweets, too, and it made him nicer, temporarily. While he was eating, he didn't bother us. So sugar became a symbol of safety and protection for me. It not only got me high to avoid my feelings, but it made the rageaholic in the family calm down a bit. Food had a lot of meaning.

Christmas time was filled with my mom's dozens and dozens of homemade cookies and candy. I remember being so focused on eating that I blanked out the whole world. I would sit in front of the television and unconsciously eat until I couldn't eat anymore. It was ruthless back then. I would make myself feel sick. I would be in pain.

Sugar put me in a haze. It triggered this excited feeling inside of me--like adrenaline was pulsing through my veins, its incredible warmth started in the center of my stomach and spread throughout my entire body. At first, after consuming tons of sugar, life felt super sharp and in focus. It gave the illusion of safety. I'd quickly hit the peak then crash into a sugar hangover. Exhaustion would be so intense that all I wanted to do was sleep. I was delirious. The only solution to move out of this state was to sleep it off.

Whenever I've experienced sugar exhaustion, I paused my life and didn't get anything done. It's debilitating. I canceled my plans in order to eat or to recover. It hurt me to be in this state, because there was so much that I wanted to do. It affected my reliability and my integrity.

Another part of the binge eating cycle was the shame spiral. I felt so ashamed of myself for doing what I did with food. I would criticize myself and beat the crap out of myself for being so out-of-control and would swear it off, even as a kid. I'd kick myself when I was down. I'd swear that I'd never do it again. Then the next day, or the next time I became hungry, I'd do it all over again.

Before pre-school, my mother would take us to do all the grocery shopping during the day when my dad was at work. The trips to the grocery store were quiet and serene especially compared to when my dad was at home. We would leisurely go through the aisles and my mom again, had no boundaries. She would let us pick out anything we wanted, mostly processed foods or sugary sweets. The grocery store was a peaceful morning. These trips included long lingering safe strolls down quiet aisles and no yelling, just soft music over the speakers and an occasional announcement from a worker.

A trip to the store was not complete without a last stop at the bakery, where we all stood in awe in front of the pastry counter, waiting to get our free cherry chip cookies along with a ton of donuts and other pastries to go. I remember vividly the maple cream-filled long john, cherry turnovers with vanilla frosting, donuts and frog cupcakes decorated with a huge pillar of green frosting. It was like crack cocaine for kids, free-basing that frosting. Pure sugar. Heaven and hell combined.

After shopping we'd go home, prepare a big lunch and watch General Hospital at 1 p.m. I ate until I was stuffed. I remember feeling numb and safe when I would fill up my body with the foods that we bought. All I had to do to feel better was to focus on the food, the tastes and the smells and the calm would take over. All my anxiety would go away.

My brother and I were given an envelope with cash from my mom to order Domino's Pizza while she was still at work. It was basically enough money for two medium pizzas with a coupon. One pizza for my baby brother and one for me. The house was empty after school--except for me and my brother. No violence. Peace and quiet and pizza. We would sit in silence, eating and watching TV.

Pizza was also like heroin to me. It was the number one drug of choice in my food addiction with donuts as number two or cheap chemical and preservative filled Little Debbies. The additives in it would make me feel so bad after a binge. All of the detrimental and damaging side effects still would not stop me. The only answer was letting God take the wheel. I had to stop with the self-reliance, self-propulsion, self-centeredness, and wanting what I wanted when I wanted it, at any cost. I couldn't do this on my own. I had to let God in.

My Father's Restaurant Peace Pipe

My father never apologized verbally for his behavior. His form of a peace pipe was always, "Hey, do you want to go out to eat?" after a big blowout simmered down.

Sometimes it was just him and I. Sometimes the whole family. There was still some grumbling out in public as we sat in the booth waiting to order, but no violence in sight. There was no communication, just all of us silently waiting for the food to arrive. When we were actually eating, it was one of the only consistently peaceful times I spent with our father growing up.

As an adult, restaurants are still charged with an addiction vibe for me. They became a reward for myself, a way to calm down, a break from self-criticism, a soothing form of comfort and/or an instant form of gratification. Every time I leave the house, I am tempted to eat out. I used to be addicted to fast food drive-thrus. Thank God He has removed that compulsion of eating food with no nutritional value, grease and empty calories.

A Life-Threatening Addiction

In Chicago, in my mid-30s, I was heavily medicated for bipolar depression. It was the worst depression of my entire life. I had suicidal ideations and was too ashamed to go into a grocery store, because of my body weight and paranoia that people were secretly making fun of me. So I would order large amounts of delivery food, or go through drive-thrus or venture out to the local Mexican bakery to get exorbitant amounts of pastries and milk. I gained 80 pounds in 3 months. The shame I felt turned suicidal.

I plotted and planned to buy a gun to kill myself. When I got into my car to drive to the pawn shop, my phone rang and I answered it. It was a woman from the Employee Assistant Program at my day job. Immediately, the numbed out place I was in, the self-destructive spell was broken and I started crying really hard. God's Holy Spirit worked through this woman. She was my angel that day. She talked me into packing a small bag and driving to the hospital instead of the pawn shop. I promised to follow through with the new plan. I checked myself into the hospital to get help with the dangerous depression. God, through this woman, saved my life.

When I was married to an alcoholic in early 2000, I drove around hunting for places to buy food. Specifically on the hunt for donuts, cakes, sweets. I went to Winchell's Donut House to pick out a baker's dozen, then would eat as much as I could driving around while I ate. Just completely numbing out from the world, from myself and from all my uncomfortable feelings. My emotions felt life-threatening. When younger, they actually were. It was life-threatening to express my feelings as a little girl. I risked being the target of violence. "I'll give you something to cry about." I'd keep frozen inside to avoid being pinched or hit. I was still responding to life as if I were still this small hurt and helpless little girl, eating to comfort myself. I would eat to maximum capacity and then throw out the rest of the donuts, out of disgust. Sometimes I'd litter and throw everything out the window. I was a very sick woman.

Fast Forward

Earlier this year, I let go of a 14-year-old friendship then, two days later, a good friend of mine completed suicide. I was shocked, angry, sad; the grief felt out of control. The miserable food addiction reared its ugly head. I started by eating at restaurants nearly every day, then began to have expensive Doordash restaurant food delivered to my front door and gorging on sugary sweets until I practically passed out. It calmed me at first, artificially, and soothed me for a split second.

I knew I was killing myself with the food, but suddenly did not know how to stop–again. I was making desperate attempts to control the messy grief. I was trying to control my intense feelings by numbing out. Our emotions are God's gifts. They give us a lot of information. I had taken back my will instead of relying on God to help me through it.

I revisited drive-thrus, which were a form of crack to ease my pain. I would order enough food for at least two people and then eat them in my isolation tank, my car. I'd deceive the fast food worker by saying I was bringing home dinner for my family. A blatant lie. Afterward, I'd get rid of the evidence by throwing away all the cartons and bags and cups. It felt like a relief to throw containers of my binge in the trash, where it belonged.

I spent all my time obsessing on food again and my thinking was centered around plotting and planning my next binge. I would get a craving and the only way for me to find "peace" with it, I thought, was to get that food substance and eat it, binge on it. Afterward there were the same shameful feelings. The cravings were an insatiable hole I could not feel. What I did not realize is that God's love was inside me. He did not want me to continue hurting my body by abusing myself with addictive recreational eating.

I wasted expensive food again. I bought food at the grocery store with great plans on cooking and preparing healthy meals. I ended up throwing nearly all the food away. Although I had a full refrigerator, I'd still eat out at restaurants or order food in. To let food in the refrigerator go bad felt like I was out of control and bleeding financially. I was powerless over my food.

My binge eating disease gives me amnesia. I forget the tools I have from the 12-step food program, to use to stop me from acting out. I forget that God is with me at all times and that I can hand over everything to Him. To surrender the cravings, my plans–to Him. The disease of addiction tricks you into thinking you don't have a disease.

Addiction, no matter which one, says, "I want what I want when I want it." That's a lot of I, I and I. The 12 step is a "WE" program. We have to let others in. We have to let God in. We cannot do this on our own. God is the answer. Only God can heal us and give us freedom from active addiction.

Consequences of Powerlessness Over the Disease of Food Addiction

As part of my step work in a 12-step program for compulsive overeaters, I wrote down 25 ways I am powerless over the first compulsive bite. Some were extremely embarrassing to admit. This exercise got me out of denial and helped show me how I CANNOT control the binge foods and binge behaviors. I had to surrender them to God and do the next best indicated step.

One day when I was writing, I got divine guidance to make a list. I read back through it after my brainstorm. It was a real eye opener.

25 things that show I am powerless over food right now:

- I went from $4,500 to $6,100 in debt on my credit card over a 3-month timeframe.
- If I put a food delivery app on my phone, I will spend an exorbitant amount on expensive food. The highest charged amount for one meal was $156.00.
- My car is filthy inside with containers and food stuck to the interior. I have a garbage bag full of fast food containers in the trunk
- I can hardly walk around the block…my legs hurt, my knees, it's hard to breathe.
- My breathing is shallow with all the extra weight I'm carrying.
- I have gained 5 pounds in the past month.
- Once I start eating sugar, the cravings keep piling on top of each other, and I cannot stop eating it.
- Food is on my mind all the time.
- I postpone or reschedule plans when I am about to pass out from eating.
- I wear a size 24x.
- I am embarrassed to go swimming because of my big body. I love swimming laps. I feel intense shame for what I've done to myself. Then the eating begins again.
- I don't like my body.

- I buy food from the grocery store and it rots in my refrigerator as I spend more money on restaurant food.
- I can't go hiking or on long walks like I used to.
- I cannot go zip-lining or skydiving, which I would like to do.
- I stop myself sometimes from socializing or going out because I am ashamed of my size.
- I move slower.
- It hurts to get in and out of my car.
- I choose over and over again to "reward" myself with sickening sweets instead of buying something like flowers or a pedicure for myself. Eating has become everything.
- I don't have extra money to pursue interests such as pottery or guitar class.
- It hurts to get comfortable in bed and hard to get out of bed.
- I have so much tension in my shoulders and neck from running from my feelings—that's where the stuck energy is at—in my shoulder and necks.
- I am so afraid to feel hungry that I am always consumed with looking ahead for what to "arrange" to eat next.
- I center my socializing around going to restaurants because it's the only "comfortable" place to be when I'm out in the world.
- My whole life is closing in on me like blinders on a horse.

When living in Chicago, I started going to Overeaters Anonymous meetings in 2008. After weeks of not really communicating with my first OA sponsor, I asked him for feedback on how to overcome my addiction to drive-thrus. He told me, "Congratulations! Your question is an act of surrender! Show's you are open, willing and honest about getting better."

He told me if I wanted to go to get fast food--to get a quick fix, that I could go in and order whatever I wanted but that I would just eat the food inside the restaurant instead of in my isolation tank (my car). That stopped the pattern of acting out via drive-thrus. Previously, I HAD to go through a drive-thru every single time that I went out.

I went to another OA meeting in Denver while living with my family again. I didn't like it. I was too ashamed to talk about it. I found flaws with everyone there. I never went back. I wasn't ready.

I switched to a daily telephone meeting. This appealed to me because nobody could see that I was overweight. It was a relief to hear from others on the phone line, sharing in real-time what was going on with them. I also used the phone to call fellow members–talking to people one-on-one, getting to know them and giving and receiving support. One lady told me about something that helped her–she made a menu plan on what to eat the next day, the night before and sent it to her sponsor. Then the next day, she would just follow it. She offered to receive my menu if I wanted to try this. I emailed her my food plan to her the day before. I did it for 3 days--I emailed my food plan to her the night before and it worked! I did not have this pressure of figuring out what to eat when I was hungry. I did not sway. It was already planned out. I could just follow the plan. I could think and focus on other things! I was abstinent for 3 days. Then I abruptly stopped. I still wanted to do it my way. I wasn't ready to surrender.

In late December 2017, at an OA meeting I wrote down the phone number of a woman who had a graceful gentle voice. She said she was available to sponsor. I loved hearing her shares. I wanted what she had, and that's exactly what you look for in a sponsor: to ask someone who has what you want. It is the best form of inspiration. I called her. I nervously asked her to be my sponsor. She said yes.

I was a chronic relapser at that point and I shared my fear that she would ditch me or fire me as a sponsee. She assured me that "We don't shoot our wounded." I was certainly wounded in more ways than one. I felt like a soldier who had survived the front lines of a 40-year war. She taught me not to beat myself up, telling me to "put down the sledgehammer and pick up a feather. She has stuck by my side through thick and thin ever since. It has been one of the most important relationships in my life, and continues to be strengthened by our journey with God and the 12 steps. She called sponsorship a trinity–you, me and God.

I was going to a ton of meetings and staying in touch with my sponsor and others in the group. I started working the steps even though I was afraid of commitment. I was afraid of letting this addiction go. It had been my companion for so long. It's a monster disguised as a friend. A part of the enemy's lies. A massive distraction.

I prayed for the willingness to be willing to hand it over to God. I prayed for the willingness to be willing to work a 12-step program around the food to the best of my ability, to work with a sponsor and to feel my feelings, to find a healthier way of handling reality. I prayed and prayed, yet I still was taking back my will and thinking I had to do it my way, that I didn't need any help from God. or others This was a huge lie that was keeping me sick.

Earlier this year, a close friend of mine died by completing suicide. It totally floored me. I didn't want to feel the tremendous grief and pain that I had inside of me. So, I turned to the old coping skill of recreational eating to numb out the pain.

Eating sugary sweets as opposed to not, is like night and day. Misery vs. serenity. Experiencing food neutrality is such a relief to my body and mind. To prepare my own food is so nurturing and my body loves fresh healthy foods. Not obsessing on food frees up my energy to use on other things that have nothing to do with food. I can treat myself in other ways too. To a pedicure, some office or art supplies, some theater, a swim.

I have to stay vigilant. The disease is "doing push ups in the parking lot," looking for a way to edge its ugliness back into my life. If I started relying on self-will alone, I could fall back into addictive behavior. I must rely—listen, ask and pray to do God's Will. This means having a strong prayer and meditation life. I can have a conversation with God; I can talk to Him during prayer time and hear Him during my stillness.

I cannot take that first compulsive bite—otherwise it's down the rabbit hole again. Day after day of feeling all alone and trying so desperately to control something I am powerless over, always leads to more powerlessness. It is a ruthless and insatiable hunger that cannot be filled because at the end of the day, it doesn't even have anything to do with the food. It's a space in me that needs self-love and trust and faith in God. It's an out-dated coping mechanism that does not serve me or others.

I do a lot of service work and I have a phone list a few miles long of great 12-step program people to call. Some of my closest inner circle friends I met in the rooms.

The program works if you work it. And if it does not work for you, I'd encourage you to reflect on how honest you are willing to be with yourself.

When I make phone calls to my fellows before I act on taking that first compulsive bite, I abandon ship and do not overeat. It happens 100 percent of the time. It is part of my personal solution to staying sober. The problem is when the thoughts get into my head that "nothing is going to stop me" from doing it, so then I don't pick up the phone…at all. So, my next move is to ALWAYS check in with God. To allow myself to feel and to pray for help. To express myself. To feel the craving and not act on it. It's amazing how I do that so well with the sex and drug addiction, and relapse on this old behavior of eating.

Shout Out for Your Help

I would really love your help. I am giving a big call out for prayers—that if you could say a prayer for me to stay sober from all addictive behaviors, even the oldest one—the only periodically active one at this point—the food addiction, that would be excellent and greatly appreciated. A simple prayer such as:

"God, please keep grant Lisa Jo freedom. Keep her emotionally sober."

Get creative even—make it as simple or as elaborate and detailed as you want. Let this be your invitation to let the ink flow. Get in touch with action words and with the poetry that is in your heart.

For tips on how to write your own prayers, see chapter 13.

There is safety in a prayer. Praying for someone is a tremendous act of care and love. It is asking God, the Almighty Creator of the Universe, to help this person. It is also humbling to experience someone praying for you. It feels good. Whenever someone speaks a prayer over me, I feel a warmth, an unconditional care and compassion from an all-loving God with His Holy Spirit working through the generous loving person praying. Hearing someone pray over me, grows my faith. It makes that little mustard seed start expanding, growing. When I hear the conviction in a person's voice or intention–the healing prayers seem miraculously and solidly possible. Faith in God is reflecting from the prayer warrior to me. It's priceless. Timeless. Surpasses all obstacles of doubt, negativity and disbelief. Prayers from others strengthen me and make me realize I am not alone and there are people in addition to God on my side, rooting for me and wanting the best for me.

Praying for someone is one of the greatest gifts you can give that person. Speaking from the heart, anointed by your faith–in written word or spoken word–is a beautiful act of loving care. Thanks to everyone ahead of time who will say a prayer for me. Miracles abound and I am open to receiving them.

I'd love to hear from you. Feel free to contact me. My phone number is: 720-326-1972. I can't promise you I'll always be able to pick up, but do me a favor–speak your prayer into a voicemail or read it into the phone. Read me other prayers you have written, too. Share your two-way prayers. Inspire me! Perhaps some day we can even pray together.

Prayers help keep us all sober. We can all use a prayer, right? I know I can! I believe you can, too! Always!

I am praying for the willingness to be willing, one day at a time, to stay out of the food addiction. To obtain true solid freedom, by the grace of God.

In Matthew 18:19 in The Passion Translation (TPT):
"Receive this truth: Whatever you forbid on earth will be considered to be forbidden in heaven, and whatever you release on earth will be considered to be released in heaven. Again, I give you an eternal truth: If two of you agree to ask God for something in a symphony of prayer, my heavenly Father will do it for you."

When I read or hear your prayers, that is us asking for something in a symphony of prayers, even if we are not praying it at once or at the same time. We are still in agreement with those beautiful positive healing prayers of freedom from all addiction and with all of God's favor.

God bless all of you. Thanks for the positive prayers ahead of time.

Don't forget–you are a phenomenal human being. There is hope. For happiness, for God's healing, for Divine Grace and second chances, or hundreds of chances. Weeping will endure for an evening but joy will always come in the morning.

Come join me in that joy; in the freedom from bondage. If I can overcome hard drugs and sex addiction, I can overcome the food issue, too. Since God restored me to sanity in one area, He has the power to restore me in ALL areas. Which means, He has the Almighty Power to restore your sanity, too.

Because I have experienced healing, **so can you**. Let's delight in our recovery. Let's share generously what was freely given to us by always being of service to others. Let's give glory to God. Let's praise Him no matter what stage we are at. No matter what is happening. Let's find the good in the world and give God the praise.

God is the answer. Lean into Him whenever you can. He wants to heal you. Meet Him with action to do the next best indicated step on your journey to wholeness. Let's do this together!

God bless you all!

References

Alcoholics Anonymous, known by most as "The Big Book."

Calming your Anxious Mind-How Mindfulness & Compassion can Free you from Anxiety, Fear & Panic by Jeffrey Brantley, MD

Mindfulness for Beginners by Jon Kabat-Zinn

Step into Action-Working the Twelve Steps of Sexoholics Anonymous

Distracted by Bob Goff

The Heart Healing Journey by Mark DeJesus

Prayers I've written from my heart to yours:

Writing my Story Prayer	4
Blessed with Connection Prayer	18
Dial the Phone Prayer	20
Admitting Powerlessness Prayer	24
Rigorous Honesty Prayer	28
Blessing a Sponsor Prayer	33
God's Hope Prayer	40
Going to a Meeting Prayer	43
Life on Life's Terms Prayer	47
Raise the White Flag Prayer	50
Half Measures Availed Us Nothing Prayer	57
Back From Relapse Prayer	68
Releasing Resistance and Rebellion Prayer	77
Untying the Knots of Resentment Prayer	79
Fear Inventory Prayer	83
The Gifts of Confession Prayer	88
Make Me Ready Prayer	97
Humility to Let Go and Let God Prayer	103
Willingness to Make Amends Prayer	109
Taking Responsibility Prayer	116
The Discipline of Spiritual House Cleaning Prayer	120
Conscious Contact with God Prayer	136
Being of Service Prayer	148
Sweet Sleep and Gratitude Prayer	159
Healing Spiraling Shame Prayer	162
Anxiety and Depression Prayer	164

Stay in Today Prayer   167
Tools of the Program Prayer   169
Lead me to Serenity Prayer   171
Faith Without Works is Dead Prayer   172

About the Author

L isa Jo Barr is a survivor and advocate, who has courageously overcome addictions to substances and behaviors such as cocaine, food, nicotine, sex, and love. Since her transformative journey began in 2007, she's been an active participant in 12-step recovery programs. She is the author of three self-published poetry books. She has written several compelling articles, columns, and OP-EDS that have been published in numerous magazines and newspapers around the world. A committed Christian, Lisa Jo credits her faith in Christ for her profound personal healing and for her perseverance in the face of adversity. Leveraging her expertise gained from five years working in the mental health field, she is deeply passionate about aiding others on their journey to recovery. Lisa Jo lives in Denver, Colorado, where she serves as a living testament that healing from the profoundest depths of despair is possible.

A free ebook edition is available with the purchase of this book.

To claim your free ebook edition:

1. Visit MorganJamesBOGO.com
2. Sign your name CLEARLY in the space
3. Complete the form and submit a photo of the entire copyright page
4. You or your friend can download the ebook to your preferred device

Morgan James
BOGO™

A **FREE** ebook edition is available for you or a friend with the purchase of this print book.

CLEARLY SIGN YOUR NAME ABOVE

Instructions to claim your free ebook edition:
1. Visit MorganJamesBOGO.com
2. Sign your name CLEARLY in the space above
3. Complete the form and submit a photo of this entire page
4. You or your friend can download the ebook to your preferred device

Print & Digital Together Forever.

Snap a photo

Free ebook

Read anywhere